MW00653816

decisive
women

To: Linda,
A wonderful encouraging Soul!
Nancy

decisive women

designing decisions in 5 minutes or less

Empowering, Influential, Decisive!

Dr Nancy Fox

DR NANCY FOX with
LAURA STEWARD, SANDRA CHAMPLAIN,
and other women like you

Red Tale Fox Enterprises, Inc.
Still Pond, Maryland

Disclaimer: This book, including any portion thereof, is not intended to offer any professional, or personal advice. The information contained herein does not replace or substitute for the services of trained professionals in any field, including, but not limited to medical, behavioral services. Under no circumstances will Red Tale Enterprises, Inc. or any of its officers, directors, representatives, agents, affiliates, or contractors be liable for any special consequential damages that are associated with the use of, or the inability to use, the information or strategies communicated through this book, even if advised of the possibility of such damages. You alone are responsible and accountable for your decisions, actions and results in life by your use of this book, you agree not to attempt to hold us liable for any such decisions, actions or results, at any time, under any circumstance.

We've taken every effort to ensure we accurately represent the strategies and their potential to help you grow as an individual. However, we do not purport this is as a substitute for professional services and there is no guarantee that you will get the results you desire using the strategies discussed in this book. This book is provided for information only and no guarantees, promises, representation or warranties of any kind regarding specific or general benefits, personal growth or otherwise, have been or will be made by us. The statements in this book are simply derived by our personal experiences and/or opinions. We make no guarantees that you will achieve any particular results from our information and we are not responsible for your actions and results in life.

Published by:
Red Tale Fox Enterprises, Inc.
nancy@drnancyfox.com
drnancyfox@gmail.com
www.drnancyfox.com

Cover design: Kathi Dunn, dunn-design.com
Interior design: Dorie McClelland, springbookdesign.com

978-0-9966545-5-5 paperback
978-0-9966545-4-8 e-book
978-0-9966545-0-0 Audiobook

Dedicated to

Dorothy June Nicholson
for her courage, strength, and faith—
living her life through "trials and tribulations,"
focusing on purpose, and finding the joy, laughter,
and peace in her soul.

Acknowledgments

Acknowledgments go to:

Women in history who have taught those in the present how to flourish as women.

Leslie Petruk, Irene Tymczyszyn, and Amy Weider who shared a room with me at a conference and believed in me before I did. These three strangers, now friends, made me feel significant in their lives, valued my message, and made me laugh until my sides hurt.

Wendy Lipton-Dibner, my mentor and leader, for giving me the tools for creating a life that is aligned with my heart and my destiny while learning effective business tools.

Rick Frishman for letting me know the first book I wrote did not meet industry standards, and if I simply followed his expertise and the experts with whom he has surrounded himself, I would become the author I dreamed of being.

Roberto Candelaria for teaching me business strategies and sponsorship through his heartfelt love and appreciation of my work and me as a person.

Bruce Barbour who took my mother's memoir and created a vision for women to communicate their experiences, their determination, and their resilience for life's challenges.

Contents

Part Three: BARS: Action

Part Four: BARS: Results

Part Five: BARS: Service

Foreword

Since you've wisely picked up a book called *Decisive Women: Designing Decisions in 5 Minutes or Less*, you may be wondering about the content within and asking yourself a few questions. I suspect one of the first questions might be something like this: "If this is a book written by women *for* women, who is this *guy* writing the foreword, and what makes him even remotely qualified to do it?"

For starters, that's a great question, and I'm glad you asked. As a coach, trainer, and fellow author, my practice originally started in the area of peak performance strategies, and I eventually followed my true passion into the area of relationships. With that kind of experience and background, as you might expect, many of my clients are women. I'm not talking about just any women, either. I'm talking about amazing, incredibly talented, and very bright women. I'm talking about driven women who want to do more, be more, and have more. My clients are doctors. Lawyers. Executives. Entrepreneurs. They've walked the halls of the Pentagon and conferred with US senators. Oftentimes they're bosses or team leaders; occasionally they're the glue that holds their team together. Sometimes they're mothers or wives or occasionally ex-wives, girlfriends, or even mistresses. I write this not to violate a confidence or impress you. I write this to convey one simple fact: Since I create a safe space for them to share some of their biggest, most challenging, and oftentimes overwhelming challenges, I've earned my place at the table as one of their closest and most trusted advisors. I would never be bold, arrogant, or even foolish enough to say I completely understand women—but I will say this: I'd have to be a fool not to notice the common patterns and recurring issues.

One of the reasons that I have become such a trusted and valuable advisor is that my experience allows me to help predict, expect, and mitigate challenges before they occur. Plus, since I've been doing this for so long, chances are very good that I have some applicable experience with another client that is invaluable in resolving issues if they do arise. Infidelities. Divorces. Firings. Health crises. Unexpected deaths. These types of things have a way of bringing even the strongest and brightest among us to their knees. Even the most decisive of women struggle in the face of such uncertainty. That's when you need that trusted voice that's always in your corner the most, and because I am that voice for many of my clients, that's also what gives me the unique credibility to write this foreword.

My first thought when I heard the title of this book was that it was a great idea that would be welcomed with open arms by many of the readers who would benefit from its wisdom. From my vantage point, I've seen how women can occasionally struggle with some aspects of decision-making, and it's not because they lack the analytical acumen, expertise, or ability to make a sound and reasoned choice. Actually, it's quite the contrary. The reason that many women get temporarily stuck in "overwhelm" has nothing at all to do with any weakness or deficiency.

Ironically, it oftentimes occurs as a direct result of one of their greatest strengths or gifts.

Let me explain. A large part of what I do is teach about masculine and feminine energies or strategies. It's not about gender because, frankly, both men and women possess both masculine and feminine traits. In my opinion and experience, it's no different than using the right tool for the right job. Both have the ability to flip back and forth in order to harness exactly what they need in a given moment. Masculine energy tends to navigate the world via analysis and logic. It's all about solving problems, fixing things, and creating a result. Occasionally it can feel somewhat insensitive when you're on the receiving end of a masculine being trying to "fix" something . . . especially if that something is you.

By contrast feminine energy tends to navigate the world primarily in the realm of feelings or using emotion as her guide. This explains why women are known as the "fairer sex" and why their use of "female intuition" is such a powerful evolutionary advantage. Someone who cultivates that intuition and "gut wisdom" has a powerful advantage when she uses it. However, women sometimes don't listen to their own instincts or divine guidance system and do the opposite of what their gut tells them. I always tell my clients that I am one of the biggest male proponents for the power of female intuition. Even if I might be uncertain about a decision or have a different opinion personally, I have learned to trust and give a great deal of deference to the power of a woman's intuition. The other advantage of a more emotion-based navigational system is that feminine strategies are far superior when it comes to activities like team building, nurturing relationships, or connecting with others. If you really want to avoid self-sabotage, while performing with more elegance, effectiveness, and efficiency, it is absolutely critical to tap into the appropriate energy for the job at hand.

It is that exact gift of emotional guidance that is occasionally at the root of a challenge when it comes to making a five-minute decision. However, that does not mean the title *Decisive Women* is an oxymoron like the terms jumbo shrimp, sweet sorrow, or amicable divorce. It simply means you have an opportunity to potentially make a radical change to your life by enhancing one very learnable skill set.

I believe readers of this book will benefit greatly by the strategies enclosed so that the next time they are faced with a dilemma or a fork in the road, they'll be able to utilize Nancy Fox's BARS exercise or one of the other techniques shared in this book to arrive at a sound decision in five minutes or less. I believe you'll be inspired and impressed by the stories of raw courage and perseverance in the face of long odds. I believe you'll find encouragement in the wonderful testimonies of women who listened to their intuition . . . followed their dreams . . . or otherwise emerged victorious in some way. I also truly hope that the stories and lessons within will ignite your passion, keep you going, or empower your faith when you need it the most. I'm confident that when you add up all that value, continuing to read this book might be the easiest decision you'll ever make.

—Dave Elliott, relationship coach,
A Legendary Love for Life

Introduction

You're here. Reading this book. What do you want to hear, learn, and be? How will this book influence you? These questions are for you to answer. This is not a lesson in micro-management. It is awareness about a five-minute or less thought process that will lead you to what you desire. Yes, you *can* design a decision in five minutes or less. In fact, you *do* make decisions each and every day in less than five minutes. And yes, many of those decisions are great ones. When you don't find favor in the result of your decisions, you will find lessons that help you grow and develop. Maybe you just haven't thought of the decisions you make in this light. Maybe you need encouragement or connection with your fellow sisters from the wisdom of their experiences? This book is for you.

This book is designed to help you through your journey as a woman. Celebrate your journey. Oh, your journey isn't what you thought it would be? Or you are working on your journey? Are you hoping to avoid the pitfalls of those around you? Are you picking yourself up after a bad relationship or a plethora of choices that have not served you well? Many of us have experienced life that blindsided us. In this book you will find strategies for designing decisions. You will find women like yourself who have experienced interesting, tragic, and tough times, not necessarily brought on by the decisions *they* made or decisions of others, but by all the variables that encompass our daily lives. The women who contributed their stories share a common thread of living life through the journey with dignity and decisiveness. Their stories showcase their hearts and souls as they share a time in their lives when they chose to make a decision that would change their destiny.

The stories idea came from my belief that my mother's story (chapter 2) should be shared. I was pursuing publishing her story with Bruce Barbour, a literary agent, when he mentioned that I should open my idea to include other women's stories. I answered the question: What do I want? I wanted a book that would touch the hearts of women by the examples of strength, courage, and faith represented by my mother's story and the stories of many other women who represented those very ideals.

Both women in history and women today have broken through rules and perceptions of their roles in our society. Many women have found the courage and tenacity to redefine the culture for women. It is my honor to help women become inspired by the influential intentions of those who have come before, learn about women's issues and a process for making decisions, and hear from women who have shared their personal stories.

I took action by sending an email to many of the friends I had met at conferences, such as Move People To Action, Author 101 University, and I Can Do It. I received ten responses in ten days from women who wanted to share their stories as part of this book. The chills ran all over my body at the notion that my desire may lead to the benefit I wanted for myself and others. From there each time I was at a conference, in a store, or anywhere there were women, I talked to them to find out if they wanted to contribute to this book. They did. And I thank them.

—Dr. Nancy Fox

part one

the influential intention of women

Chapter 1

Open my eyes, find my strength

by Nancy Fox

It was my mother who told me not to wait till you're forty-something to stop letting people walk all over you. She confessed to me that she had done that very thing most of her life. I remember the conversation vividly. We were at the bank drive-through window, and it was her birthday. The teller asked her how old she was, and since she had replied "twenty-nine" so often, she momentarily could not find the truth about her age. I was ten. She was thirty-nine. She was also attempting to find truths about *herself*—that her name was Dorothy, not Vivian, which was on her birth certificate, and not Sally, the nickname given to her by her sisters.

Walking all over me? At ten years old I didn't quite understand, but at forty-something the awakening began. My children were moving into adulthood and finding their own lives. My quest for education was a larger focus than ever, and yet my physical being and mind were not participating. I was tired all of the time. My joints ached. I couldn't focus and organize the way I had previously. My dad and I had been diagnosed with Lyme disease and Babesia. Dad had been in the chair for quite some time, but I was working full-time and in college part time. I didn't have time for my body to shut down. But it did. I began a journey of confusion and disconnect that would affect my life in profound ways.

My dad's health was failing. He had heart disease. He had had a heart attack at sixty-six, the week before my college graduation. He had lived well for a while, but in the blizzard of 2010 he was near death and was flown to a heart hospital. From under the oxygen mask he said, "I love you; I'll be okay." Dad did survive that night, and the next six months of his life, for me, were the most memorable. Along with my siblings, I took care of dad *and* mom, because mom was fighting lung cancer and didn't have the strength to care for him, especially since he had become bedridden. Moving from daughter to caregiver is a transition many women face.

I found joy in the decision to care for my parents. I could have decided this was unbearable, uncomfortable, and inconvenient. A decision I made when dad's first heart attack happened was to never regret their passing from this life. A decision to be in contact with my parents at least once per week was the solution to never regret missing the time I had while they were still on earth. The wheelchair walks with dad and the many conversations with mom served me beyond my understanding. MY DECISION WORKED! Both parents died within nine months of each other, and the pain of their loss was indescribable, but I had no regrets.

After their deaths I needed to learn about the strength, love, and understanding I so effortlessly applied to my parents. I took a look at my relationships with everyone, especially with my husband. A quest to understand my interactions and focus affected everyone I met, especially those I loved. I decided to look into situations and events from the perspective of my loved ones who had shaped my present understanding.

My husband was confused about my condition of Lyme disease and Babesia. He was astounded at the cost of the treatment I was given to eradicate the chronic condition that had taken over my body and my spirit. As I struggled through the loss of executive functioning, memory lapses, and physical inabilities, he lost me and I lost him. My communication skills were significantly slowed. When we had time together, I was so fatigued I would fall asleep. Neither of us understood the symptoms of the disease that left us disconnected. While I was struggling to fire my synapses to keep them from dying from the disease, someone was desperately attempting to replace me in my husband's life. It was through the journey with him that both of us opened our eyes to what was happening to us; we found our strength and, more importantly, found our love for each other to support one another beyond our understanding.

My brain fog burned off, and I realized some of the people I was trusting were exactly the people who were not to be trusted. I was able to observe again and saw inconsistencies in the people around me. My mom's words of wisdom so many years ago began to make sense on a deeper level. I stood up, found my voice, and decided not to "suffer in silence" any longer.

A young, strong-willed girl emerged. The one who would take on the enemies of a life full of love, compassion, and joy. The one who was bullied in elementary school and who decided to please everyone in her path to avoid the pain of rejection and shed her identity would now take back her life. Did it happen all at once? Yes, to the decision! No, the transformation didn't happen all at once. Repairing years of conditioning is a conscious, ongoing effort. Step by step, observing, word by word, I found the untruths that had stopped me from being decisive and standing up for my beliefs, despite what people thought, and my choosing to be walked over. My mother's words of strength and love for self became clear to me. Moment-by-moment decisions were made with a laser focus of what I wanted in the present moment. I did consider the future and the impact my decisions would have on loved ones. But for the first time in my life, since childhood, I considered my beliefs and my desires before anyone else.

My illness set off an array of decisions about my health. From the moment I was diagnosed with a chronic illness until the day I could finally say my health was not my enemy, was a journey of seven years. I learned that I could have many labels and attach my identity to all or any one of them. I found as long as I felt significant with the next label to describe my symptoms, the more symptoms manifested themselves or fit a new label. Although not initially, I then decided not to define myself by the many labels I was given. My identity became I am healthy; I am eating well; I am energetic. Gradually, I became those statements. Does that mean I never ate anything that was detrimental to my health? Does that mean that I exercised every day? Does that mean I was consistent with all that I feel, see, and do? No, yet in a moment of decision, I reflect on the places that I have been with my health and my spirit and decide in that moment what will serve me now and in the future. I sought out many perspectives on health, diet, exercise, the immune system, and alternative methods of treating disease. Many of the lessons learned reach back to the basics of life and fueling our bodies. I have talked to several people who have followed the health path, and for some unknown reason they have still been susceptible to a disease or illness that is beyond our understanding, with no human reason for their suffering or demise.

To open my eyes, find my strength, and love beyond my understanding is a gift of my decision-making—to see, to feel, to love, and to be the person I am right now and have gratitude for the good and the challenges that lead to growth and contribution. I was comfortable before forty years old because everything was the way I had planned it, or so I told myself. It is not the number forty or any age that shapes your strength, seeing things as they are, or loving beyond your understanding. It is in the choices and the challenges where decisions emerge that shape our lives, determine our destiny, and open our eyes. Then we gain strength and love beyond our understanding.

Chapter 2

I wasn't ready yet

by Dorothy Nicholson,
told by her daughter Nancy Fox

The moment the ice water poured over my warm head, my spirit knew life would have challenges. I was six months old at the time, but that was the beginning of a mother showing me I wasn't loved. In the next four years of my young life, various incidents happened that cause most people to cringe when they hear the descriptions. Once I was taken across the road and told to hang onto a pole and not leave or sit down. I watched as my mother left to go across the road to the house. I got tired but didn't sit. She had been out of sight for so long that I walked across the road, and instantly she jumped out from the bushes. I don't recall what happened next but the next memory left scars. My mother told me to sit on the radiator (a steam heating unit). Following mother's directions, my sister went to the thermostat and turned it up. My hands and backs of my knees began to warm up and then burn as the heat became unbearable. My skin melted onto the radiator. I don't remember what happened next but my legs and hands were blistered. I remember that the doctor bandaged me up, and my mother told my father I fell down the steps. In no time at all, I was in a car with someone who took me on a long ride to my foster parents.

My foster parents were good to me. Although there were chores to do and there was a long lane to walk down to get to the bus, other girls were there. It was better than the times with my mother. I grew up having limited contact with her. She promised me a bike once, but I never saw it. Through adulthood, I searched for my mother's love by visiting her, but I wasn't able to find it.

I met a soldier when working at the Belle Haven serving as a waitress. The man was fresh, and he was told "no" several times. Once in the car, I finally told him to let me out and I would walk home. I got out of the car and walked home. He continued his pursuit of me until a friend of mine said she would double date with me and I would be okay. We dated and were later married for sixty years.

During those sixty years many decisions were made. The first was to marry Luke because I was pregnant with our first child. In those days, that is what happened most often when a girl got pregnant. Not long after Joanne was born I was pregnant with David. David had colic for six weeks. Then David was scalded by pulling a hot pot of water off the stove onto himself. Luke was accused of having a baby with another woman, and we had to pay child support. Seven years later the courts determined he was not the father. I had no place to go so I learned to cope with whatever came at me. After all, I had survived a mother's lack of love, and I was still looking for confirmation that I was loved. Luke provided for us and was not abusive. I loved him and I believed he loved me.

Along came Richard who was healthy and fun until he was diagnosed with a severe chronic ear infection that led to surgery and a loss of hearing. Then Doug was born. We moved to a farm because Luke was working to make enough money through farming. During the day he worked as an electrician and plumber. Nancy was born soon after we moved to the farm. Doug was given a ride in the manure spreader and an accident punctured his brain. He survived with a reading difficulty as a consequence of the event. Nancy had pneumonia and we almost lost her.

As the children moved into their teenage years and adulthood the transition was difficult. Within a short period of time the difficulties came in a wave of unbearable events. Joanne married an abusive husband. David murdered two people. Richard wrecked his car by running into a cow. Doug wanted to get married because his girlfriend was pregnant. Nancy decided to marry at eighteen. My children wanted to marry in their mid- to late teenage years. I had done the same and saw the trials of a young marriage with subsequent children. Somehow deep in my soul I did not want my children to follow in my footsteps, but the path was inevitable.

Joanne married an alcoholic and an abusive husband. There were many times she sought shelter at our house from the abuse. And yet I told her, "You made your bed, now lie in it." I guess you are wondering why a mother who was abused from nearly birth until age four would say that to her own daughter. She had sex with the man once and insisted that he marry her. She didn't know him. I tried to persuade her not to walk down that road, but she decided to marry him anyway. There are times a mother has to teach hard lessons about taking responsibility for the decisions and choices her child/young adult has made, helping her create new decisions based on new information. I could not help Joanne with her marriage. She had to figure out what she wanted and decide how to live her life. She got out of the marriage after twenty-six years of many incidents of living with an alcoholic who was abusive. Her abusive husband ended killing a man and dying in prison in the later years of his life.

Within a year or so, David married with Luke's and my signature because he was seventeen and determined to marry Caroline. David felt the need to get married because most of his friends were getting married. He had dropped out of school to pursue his love of farming. After eighteen months of marriage, David found his wife in bed with another woman. He was distraught, and I had to help him. I took him to a psychiatrist who gave him Valium. Within a few days policemen were at our house asking where he was. He had left with no notification a couple of days before. The policemen told my husband the news. Then as gently as possible he told me our son had killed his mother-in-law and father-in-law, and wounded his brother-in-law. I collapsed feeling overwhelmed from the shock of the information. I knew nothing would be as devastating as this. For the next year or so our names were in the paper until the trial was completed. Our children were taunted and tested. Then came the Sunday visits to the state penitentiary. How do you love someone knowing he took others' lives? I considered moving away to another state but decided to face our lives as they had unfolded. One of the most difficult times for me was to continue to bowl on the local team. The daughter of the deceased bowled in the league also. Neither one of us stopped being a member of the bowling league, as we understood that neither of us could blame the other for what happened. We decided to forgive, grieve, and be in each other's presence, as difficult as it would be.

Richard was in love with a young girl at the time when David committed murder. The parents of the young girl decided that the two should go their separate ways because they did not want their daughter involved with a family who had such tremendous troubles in their lives. Richard was heartbroken. One night driving home from her residence, Richard struck a large cow and demolished his car. He wasn't physically injured but experienced loss. At that time he had lost both of his loves, his first love, the young girl, and his second love, his Camaro.

In the midst of David's trial, Doug came home to tell us that his girlfriend was pregnant. His father and I had signed for David to get married, but I was not about to sign for Doug to get married. The difficult decision to abort the unborn child was made among the parents of the teenagers. Doug and his girlfriend ran off together and hid in a woods about forty minutes away from our home. They finally returned, and the unborn child was aborted. In the midst of the chaos, embarrassment, and trials I wasn't ready yet to give up on my life but found it difficult at times to hold my head up.

Nancy decided to marry her high school sweetheart at eighteen-years-old. After all that I had been through with my other children, I wanted more for her. She had done well in high school and had found a hard-working nice young man that her dad and I approved of for her life. But she was eighteen and could make her decisions without my consent.

Within three years she told me she was pregnant, and to be honest I wasn't as thrilled as she thought I would be.

Within months the next challenge in our family's life would be about David once again. David died by suicide while in prison, and the emotions flooded again. I just wanted to hide. It was difficult to face others, and I wondered what they were thinking. I wasn't ready yet to live through another monumental life event. At some point, all of our family made decisions to handle the feelings of these life events and continue to live our lives.

For years I had watched Billy Graham and asked God for his forgiveness, not truly understanding the forgiveness that had been bestowed upon me. Luke and I enjoyed our time together as he pursued real estate investing. That meant cleaning, painting, and polishing houses into resalable properties. Luke bought a campground as an investment, working it for seven years until it finally took the life out of him. When that was sold he seemed to lose his Energizer Bunny® ability and slowed down to a crawl. He rarely got out of the lounge chair. In December, I was diagnosed with stage-four lung cancer. A nodule located next to the aorta was cancerous. They removed it. With faith that I would recover from the consequences of fifty years of smoking, the next several years were difficult at times. Chemotherapy, radiation, a second surgery, and the wait every three months for "good numbers" encompassed my life. Fixing meals and taking care of Luke was my job, my desire, and my service from the time we were married. I lived to love my husband and my children and enjoy my grandchildren and great grandchildren. At times, over the next nine years, I was unable to take care of Luke the way I had taken care of him all of our years of marriage. It troubled me not to be there for him. During that time he showed me sweet love by taking care of me and talking to me in a loving voice. I wasn't ready yet for us to be separated in life or death.

February 2010 was a winter to remember on the east coast. Luke had a heart attack, and only one-lane roads led to the hospital, so he was flown to a heart hospital. I could not bring myself to go to the hospital. I knew I was losing him. He returned to me with intense care needs, and I rejoiced in the fact he was with me. We had the children coming in to help us both, along with caregivers and hospice workers. For the first time in our lives I saw Luke cry when he realized his life would be shortened and he could do nothing about missing his children and me. He professed his love for the children and me in his gentle voice. I knew I was loved. I decided to move to a smaller place with Luke for practical reasons, not realizing I would miss my home as much as I did. I also didn't realize that I wouldn't be protected in the small apartment from the gradual loss of the love of my life. I made the decision that Luke would move to a nursing home just up the street from the apartment. He asked about me and for me often. A week later he died. I wasn't ready yet.

For the next two months I wandered aimlessly. My children, family members, and friends were there, but no one could fill the void in my soul. Then Nancy called to invite me to live with her. I immediately said yes! Nancy had bought the family farm, so it was as if I was going home. During the months until Christmas I grieved but began to remember the many memories in the home Luke and I had lived in for twenty-six years while raising our family. We had Christmas dinner and all the children came. We made donuts that I used to make when the kids were little in the same kitchen. Somehow the donuts were not as savory as the treat we remembered. We laughed at how the time had passed and our memories were sweeter than the donuts.

I was told in February that the numbers were not good, and that I didn't have any options. I told the doctor I had lived a good life. I was given medication to keep me comfortable. Again my family members, friends, and my best friend Agnes took care of me. In April I saw the caregiver costs and decided it was too much to pay for my care. I fired everyone except for Agnes. After all I had just turned eighty, and I certainly could decide how much money to spend on my care. I wasn't ready yet.

I took the next several weeks to reflect on my life, my relationships, and my trials and tribulations. I reflected on the people who had stayed with me throughout my life's journey and those who didn't for the reasons that served them. In May, I felt weaker by the day and began to tell my family members I was tired. The doctor had told me he couldn't predict whether my death would be violent or not. One day I woke up, looked at the person in front of me and said, "You're new." My daughter unwrapped the towel from her head and then I said, "Oh, I don't even know my own daughter." We laughed and talked together. She left to go to a doctor's appointment when my caregiver came. Others came that day to sit with me, my friend Agnes, my grandson, granddaughter, Katie the hospice nurse, Bob the social worker, and my daughter. Before I took my last breaths, my daughter told me she was ready for me to be received into God's arms. I was ready, and I knew I was loved.

Chapter 3

Influential women in history

by Nancy Fox

"Women, like men, should try to do the impossible. And when they fail, their failure should be a challenge to others."
Amelia Earhart

Women in history inspire us and make us think—we admire the gifts that were given to them. This chapter highlights a few of the many women who have made life for others a bit simpler. They are noted for a moment of decision or a lifetime of decisions that changed the landscape of the world as they knew it.

If we could see in their mind's eye, we might see a thought process of how a woman may do whatever she wants to do. We might see how she shared inspiration with others through words so that the communication of womanhood is ongoing. Some may have chosen to teach their women counterparts about the era in which they lived, while others may have looked into the future to save the next generation from the struggles of the past. Whatever purpose drove these influential women, our lives today are humbled by their contributions and inspired by their courage and decisiveness.

Here is a partial list of women who lived during 1500–1940 with the approximate date of their contribution. The societal norms of their time reflect their courage. It is a tribute to these women that their strengths were recognized in the midst of their quest to eradicate the imposed societal limitations.

Entertainment
Annie Oakley (1885), Katharine Hepburn (1932)

Politics
Joan of Arc (1429), Virginia Claflin Woodhull (1872), Clare Boothe Luce (1953)

Literature
Mary Katherine Goddard (1766), Louise May Alcott (1852), Harriet Beecher Stowe (1852), Louise Nevelson (1922)

Art
Edmonia Lewis (1864), Grandma Moses (1934), Georgia O'Keeffe (1920), Frida Kahlo (1932)

Human rights
Harriet Tubman (1845), Isabella Beecher Hooker (1877), Rosa Parks (1955), Helen Keller (1904)

Innovation and leadership
Sacajawea (1805), Biddy Mason (1850), Margaret Getchell (1861), Ellen Shallow Richards (1870), Sarah E. Goode (1885), Amelia Earhart (1932)

Public service
Florence Nightingale (1854), Clara Barton (1861), Jane

Addams (1887), Eleanor D. Roosevelt, (1940s), Anne Sullivan (1886)

Prior to 1940, women in history reflect the restrictions of available opportunities. Despite the constraints, those women influenced others by their decisions to pursue their passions. I am positive that women were intricately involved in many other facets of life and careers but may not have been noted or reported due to the era in which they lived. Many of their biographies reflect the social expectations and norms of the time period, including marriage. The belief that women were homemakers with the sole purpose to find a husband and raise children significantly impacted their view of themselves and their opportunities to explore their gifts of intelligence, creativity, and being designers of their destiny. In spite of the norms of the era, some women had the passion to pursue the desires of their hearts. The women with significant contributions prior to 1940 were role models for the women who experienced new opportunities in the last century.

Women today have a tremendous opportunity to learn from inspiring women in the past, to communicate via internet connections and social media with influential women of the present, and to connect with women all around them who are their mentors, colleagues, family members, or friends. Let us not relinquish the incredible opportunity to find, follow, and friend a woman with integrity, grit, and experience that will hold us up or lead us to our destiny.

Chapter 4

Influential women today

by Nancy Fox

"Think like a queen. A queen is not afraid to fail. Failure is another stepping stone to greatness." Oprah Winfrey

The baby boomer generation revolutionized belief systems for society and for themselves. People who were born from 1946–1964 became 40 percent of the population by 1965. Having a significant status in the general population brought forth a momentum of rule changers. To meet the basics needs of baby boomers, neighborhoods evolved into suburban developments; fast food chains appeared, beginning with McDonald's in 1948 and then Burger King, Taco Bell, Wendy's, Carl's Jr., KFC, and Jack in the Box during the1950s. Eating out rather than eating well-cooked meals from the "woman of the house" became more popular. The routine of the nightly family dinner table changed—freeing women from the kitchen and the notion that women must have certain duties in the home. The change was gradual and at times created controversy over women's changing roles due to past belief systems that were resistant to change.

At the time of this publication, the women listed below have influenced the overall perception of women. In the last fifty years, the rules for women have been broken. Diversity has emerged in the roles for women. Overall, no longer are women considered one dimensional or traditional. The narrow concept of women as homemakers, wives, and mothers—and sometimes as certain kinds of employees—has changed as women are making a difference in the world. Many of the firsts for women have been filled. The diversity of women in the forefront of business, sports, and entertainment is a vast contrast from the time prior to the 1940s. Women have been introducing themselves to the business world, running businesses, and mixing diversity into our culture. The job women can have and the way women express themselves has been unfolding over the last fifty years. Are there still challenges for equality? Yes! However, women have taken the initiative to design their careers through entrepreneurship and take charge of their own financial success. The following women (and organizations) have shown us that women are multidimensional, unique, and contribute to the greater good. They are representative of the many who have influenced and lead the revolution for women to choose their destiny.

Entertainment

Aretha Franklin, Joan Rivers, Oprah Winfrey, Taylor Swift, Beyonce, Whitney Houston, Dolly Parton, Angelina Jolie, Meryl Streep, Lady Gaga, Adele, Avril Lavine

Politics

Indira Ghandi, Michele Obama, Margaret Thatcher, Queen Elizabeth II, Hillary Clinton, Condoleezza Rice

Literature

Maya Angelou (*I Know Why the Cage Bird Sings*), Betty Friedan (*The Feminine Mystique*), Harper Lee (*To Kill a Mocking Bird* and *Go Set a Watchman*), Toni Morrison (*Beloved*), J. K. Rowling (Harry Potter series), Danielle Steel (*Going Home*), Amy Tan (*The Joy Luck Club*), Rachel Abbott (*Only the Innocent*)

Art

Faith Ringgold, Tracey Emin, Kara Walker, Helen Frankenthaler, Berenice Abbott

Sports

Delle Donne, Serena Williams, Ghoncheh Ghavami, Tatyana McFadden, Carina Vogt, Lindsey Vonn, Mia Hamm, the 2015 US women's soccer team

Health

Evelyn Lauder (breast cancer awareness activist), Helen Mayo MD, Women and Babies Health Association—Australia

Psychology

Dr. Ruth (sex therapist), Sherry Turkle (technology professor), Cloé Madanes

Innovation and leadership

Helen Gurley Brown (*Sex and the Single Girl*), Maria Goeppert-Mayer, Marissa Mayer (Yahoo CEO), Sally Ride (first woman astronaut in space), and many more

Chapter 5

The feminine controversy

by Nancy Fox

"The modern woman is the curse of the universe. A disaster, that's what. She thinks that before her arrival on the scene no woman ever did anything worthwhile before, no woman was ever liberated until her time, no woman really ever amounted to anything." Adela Rogers St. Johns

A cultural change has allowed women to move into masculine roles, to push against their male counterparts to fit in and work alongside them, and to eventually take some of their positions. Beyond the 1940s, women have taught their daughters, granddaughters, nieces, and girls they influence through organizations to believe in possibilities.

Along with this cultural shift came controversy. Controversy inspires, challenges, and erupts emotions from the various belief systems engaged in long-term preservation. Women have been judged, criticized, and occasionally celebrated for their contributions in art, history, executive roles in corporations, and society. In that lies risk-taking, when women decisively determine their strength to endure and see their ideas, work, and contributions emerge. Women in their feminine role are to be sensitive and gentle, working from the right sides of their brains, not like the detail-oriented, decisive leaders working from the left sides of their brains. In the past women were categorized into a section of humanity based on their roles in society. The introduction of "sleeping to the top" emerged. Women were/are judged on using the feminine sides to influence men to give them positions in the company based on sexual favors, and sometimes these judgments have often come from women themselves.

Today the controversy lies in the portrayed roles of women in entertainment, such as books, storylines, or other forms of media. In her review of the 2015 movie *Cinderella,* Elizabeth Girvan explains how our perceptions of a feminine woman continues the controversy of what makes women feminine and defines their level of ability or strength. According to Girvan, "Disney is not the problem. The problem is that society holds a skewed perception of strong women. We are taught, as women, that we must choose between being a badass and a ball gown enthusiast. Not only is this wrong, but it is dangerous. To insist that characters like Cinderella are not representations of strong women (simply because they wear glass slippers) is to dismiss femininity as a quality of strength."[1]

In 2015 Ronda Rousey, bantamweight champion, UFC®, demonstrated toughness and established ultimate athlete status and femininity woven throughout her journey. Many have come before her and lived the ups and downs of popularity and admiration. The level of notoriety may be a measure of impact for Ronda and women who may question their femininity and their identity when faced with challenges of loss, whether the loss is competitive, physical, emotional, or spiritual. Women can be anything they choose in life as long as they find their core being and live from that point. Being the true design you were intended to be rather than hiding behind the mask of someone else's expectations is the best exemplary way to be feminine no matter the circumstance.

In her book *Femininity*, Susan Brownmiller describes what femininity is not: "Whimsy, unpredictability, and patterns of thinking and behavior that are dominated by emotion, such as tearful expressions of sentiment and fear, are thought to be precisely because they lie outside the established route to success."[2] Admit it, women may be quick to comfort another woman when expressing emotions, or to judge them for their "drama" inducing personalities. To balance the strong successful woman with the feminine (perceptions or reality) is a slight of hand as one moves through her day.

In an article written by Anna Pasternak for MAILONLINE entitled "Fast track to femininity: Why competing with men has left women out of touch with their feminine side," Anna's friend Sophie said, "'I have absolutely no idea how to be a woman any more,' she says. 'Because I run my business, my home and make all the decisions about the boys, I feel totally unfeminine.'"[3] The controversy between women with careers and their ability to stay feminine with all the demands continues to confuse women with which side to stand. I believe women have shown the masses that there doesn't necessarily need to be a controversy. Women have moved through the last few decades showing that they can find the balance of womanhood and success. Is it easy? It is less of a controversial subject as women emerge with different expectations for themselves and for their sisters. Julia Serrano approached the controversy of femininity this way:

> In our culture, a trait is deemed "feminine" if it is often associated with women. Common examples include being verbal and communicative, emotive or effusive, being nurturing and having an appreciation for beautiful or aesthetically pleasing things. Similarly, other traits are deemed "masculine" solely because they are often associated with men (being competitive or aggressive, physical exertion or using brute force, being silent and stoic and being mathematically or technically oriented). What all of these traits share is the fact that they are all *human traits* that are found to varying degrees in all people regardless of their gender. Most of us express some combination of traits from both the feminine and masculine categories.[4]

If we simply look at the scientific data about the behaviors of women through the lens of masculine or feminine, then we miss the very essence of women. Women are living beings designed by their culture and experiences. Simply put, the quest for understanding women from looking at the desegregated data of our differences may create a path of looking for the differences within ourselves and other women, therefore defeating the purpose for understanding. If we simply look for each woman's purpose and beauty within her soul we may find our similarities as women and embrace our differences.

Females are wired to express feminine traits but have masculine traits as well. The discovery of women having a mixture of traits deemed feminine and masculine provides a deeper understanding of women. This mixture of traits has evolved as women have claimed their true identity by unleashing the perspectives and rules of the past to become the influential women they design themselves to be. The societal input of what is expected from women continues to evolve as the personal and professional roles of women move into the future. The belief each woman has for herself regarding her femininity is her design based on an understanding of relationships with self, other women, and men.

Chapter 6

Feminine energy

by Katrina Tse Elliott

"Any time women come together with a collective intention, it's a powerful thing. Whether it's sitting down making a quilt, in a kitchen preparing a meal, in a club reading the same book, or around the table playing cards, or planning a birthday party, when women come together with a collective intention, magic happens." Phylicia Rashad

I feel blessed to be able to contribute a chapter on understanding the feminine. My personal journey has been a very difficult one at times, but it has been a blessing in disguise because it helped me reach a greater understanding of the feminine. That would not have been possible without some help along the way. I owe a great debt of gratitude to some of the coaches who showed me the way at times, including Anthony Robbins, Alison Armstrong, John Demartini, Saida, Brene Brown, John Gray, and David Deida. It is an honor to share and contribute my own story, as well as recommend the work of others I respect and appreciate.

When we are born, we are born with a core masculine or core feminine. Just because we are born a girl, doesn't mean our core is feminine energy (although, in the majority of cases, that is the case). The same holds true for men and the masculine.

As I went through my life as a child, I experienced a number of childhood traumas including sexual assaults, abandonment, and violence in the home. Left to navigate these crises on my own, I learned to use a number of protective masks as a coping mechanism. For me, the tough girl mask was certainly the most popular. This worked well as a strategy to cope with the world as a wounded girl. I joined the police and became a lawyer. I married and tried for six years to have a baby with many unsuccessful attempts at in vitro fertilization. I was core feminine on the inside; however, I was very masculine in my exterior. My first husband was a wonderful man, however, while he was core masculine, he was somewhat externally feminine in his mannerisms.

I had been doing a large amount of personal development and asked a question of a colleague one day: "If I can attract anything in my life, then why can't I attract a baby into my life?" He answered simply, "Because a man can't have a baby." Wow . . . in that moment of truth, I experienced a profound breakthrough. My life changed forever that day. From that moment on, I started on a quest to have a look at the energy that I was creating and sharing with others. I became far more conscious of how I was showing up in the world.

Over the next six years I split up with my husband, got retrenched from my career, and found a goddess role model. In that time, I also discovered the best-selling book, *Eat Pray Love* by Elizabeth Gilbert, about a woman who set off on a journey of self-discovery after a particularly difficult breakup. Inspired by the book—and my own painful breakup—I also set off on an open-ended, around-the-world trip. I really didn't have a specific agenda or itinerary in mind. I just knew I wanted to pursue my passion for travel, and I wanted to study the art of femininity and master letting go at the same time. That open-ended trip eventually stretched into a four-year journey of self-discovery and empowerment. When it finally ended, I had made some huge, life-changing shifts. And those shifts made all the difference when I finally met my now-husband at a personal development event in the United States. He is a relationship coach, and together we are blessed to travel the world in order to touch, move, and inspire others to create the love for life that we now share.

Removing the mask

As we travel through life, we tend to wear many masks. Women and girls, especially, learn to do this at a very young age. Sometimes we hide our wounds behind the mask of the "tough girl." Sometimes we take on the role of the "damsel in distress" in order to be rescued and prove to ourselves that someone cares. Sometimes we wear the mask of the "drama queen" in order to test others just to see if we're actually "safe"—which just happens to be the number one need of the feminine.

The problem with wearing these types of masks is that it actually prevents others from seeing us for who we really are in our core. It shields us from any sort of real vulnerability or authenticity. It keeps us trapped behind a facade and out of integrity. It also prevents us from doing the personal discovery it takes to uncover our own true voice.

Women quite often throw themselves into their roles. They get lost in their roles as mom to their children. They lose their identity in marriages to their spouse. Sometimes, they get immersed in their careers and the pursuit of various goals. The tragedy is that in this process, they become busy *doing* instead of *being*. They put others as priorities in front of themselves and mistake selfishness for self-nurturing.

After coaching many women, it appears that by the time the end of the day comes, they are exhausted and fall into bed, only to start it all over again the very next day. I have found that many women believe that vulnerability is a weakness. The truth is—real vulnerability is the ultimate strength because it strips away the masks and actually dares to get real. If you think that's easy, you've probably never tried it. To understand this game-changing concept even better, I recommend you look into the work of Brene Brown, today's leading academic researcher studying the effects of shame and vulnerability.

The feminine is really about embracing flow and flexibility. It's about owning your vulnerability and mastering the art of letting go. It's learning to trust that the universe will always provide for you. Feminine is really about a way of being, and it's important to remember that males can tap into their feminine energy also, especially if they need to connect.

Feminine navigates the world through emotion. She responds through intuition and gut feelings. It is such a shame that many women ignore their intuition, override their own wisdom, and find themselves in hot water later. Occasionally, her decisions may appear illogical, and that confuses the masculine.

I love a wonderful line that Jack Nicholson once delivered in his movie called *As Good as It Gets.* When an adoring female fan asks him "How do you write women so well?" he says, "I think of a man, and I take away reason and accountability. . . ." I think that sums it up in a nutshell.

Masculinity is about accountability, logic, trust, and respect. The question is in which energy do you spend most of your time, and is it serving you and your relationship? A great example that Alison Armstrong (from Understand-Men.com) teaches is when the masculine needs a couch moved from one room to the other, he figures out the best way to take action and not waste energy. He calls his friend, gives him simple directions with no wasted words, and the task is soon completed. Meanwhile, the feminine energy fluffs the pillows to make it pretty while its being carried and then offers to make coffee and bake biscuits in order to nurture and take care of her movers. Now these are extreme examples and it's important to remember that both genders possess both energies. However, it's also important to remember that when you over rely on and overuse your noncore energy, over time, there is a cost to be paid.

Ladies, I know you may be saying, "I am a successful business women, or I am in a management role, so how do I become more feminine?" (Remember, I was a police sergeant and lawyer. I know it's not easy sometimes.) This is a very common question asked by a lot of frustrated, overwhelmed women. Be warned. If you lead from the masculine constantly, it will cause you to feel burned out and attract feminine men or flip the polarity in your relationship (which will affect your attraction to your partner). Too much testosterone in the body also is linked to health implications including adrenal burnout, and in some cases, infertility.

The key

If you want to re-embrace your feminine energy, self-awareness is the first step. You have to become more aware of how you're showing up—not to mention, what you really want. I spend a lot of time connecting with myself and loving me for who I am. I have spent thirty days in silence in an ashram in India and observing myself of who I am. Traveling the world solo was also a wonderful and insightful experience.

Seek coaches and role models and ask for help. I have a friend who married a most feminine Russian woman. She is a great wife, devoted mother, and successful businesswoman. She coached me for many hours on how to embrace my femininity. I remember walking out one day, wearing a gorgeous dress, flower in the hair, crystal jewelry on, and she took one look and said "my work is done." I feel very blessed to be connected to this soul sister, and, of course, I pay it forward with other women when they need guidance too.

Rituals are important. Although I am retired as a police officer and lawyer, I am now a property investor, so I am consciously aware of sitting in masculinity. I fill my day with rituals of filling my queen tank so I can share my best version of myself with my new husband, family, and friends. I nurture my body with wonderful healthy food, wear essential oils, take baths, and wear sexy underwear, even under my renovation clothes.

I have a belief system that says no matter what happens, the cause is in the future and the universe is always there to support me. I meditate daily and, at times, ask the universe to guide me where I need to be in a given moment. I have never been let down yet. When I was on my "Eat Pray Love" journey, I practiced the art of letting go on a regular basis. I learned to get quiet and go within in order to be guided. The more I did this, the more I felt protected, connected, and directed. This was not easy and it took some time and practice. At one time, I pursued my top two needs of significance and certainty on a constant basis, and the day I finally decided to change that, everything began to shift for the better.

I hope that sharing my experiences has created some value for you and allows you to make some new choices that will more effectively serve you in getting to where you want to go sooner rather than later. Nothing makes me feel better than to be blessed to touch, move, and inspire women from all around the globe, so that they can be the best version of themselves in this lifetime.

Chapter 7

The science behind decision-making

by Nancy Fox

"If I had to live my life again, I'd make the same mistakes, only sooner." Tallulah Bankhead

The debate of having emotion intertwined with decision-making has influenced the perception of women and their ability to be effective decision-makers. In the past, women were considered poor decision-makers. Evidence of that is the old comment "women are indecisive," which led to a belief that women *are* indecisive. The idea that women are emotional and therefore cannot make good decisions under the "spell" of emotions was adopted. Once this idea was said and repeated, the belief emerged that women are indecisive, and some cultures adopted the belief to pass on to future generations. Since some qualitative data supports perceptions of women having indecisive qualities, a look at quantitative data is essential to dispel any misconceptions of the decision-making capability of women.

Cognitive disciplines have established definitions for decision-making based on the focus of the discipline. In psychology, decision-making is seen as a cognitive process. The process begins with belief and values or a response that leads to a choice, but not necessarily an action that creates a result. Deciding to buy a gym membership or a learning program does not necessarily lead to using the gym membership or learning the program that was purchased. In neuroscience, decision-making is based on chemical and electrical connections within the brain when a person is presented with options. Recent brain research about decision-making has shown specific coordination of the brain systems or parts that lead to a decision.

Behind every great idea is science to support or refute it. The art of decision-making is found in the plethora of research on brain function, emotional connection, and other influential factors. Recent brain research has shown new information that links the decision-making process to key areas of the brain. These key areas include the frontal lobe, prefrontal lobe, prefrontal cortex, hypothalamus, orbitofrontal cortex, anterior cingulate cortex, basal ganglia, amygdala, the nucleus accumbens, the limbic system, and a host of electrical and chemical communications. The combination of information and coordination among these influential contributors impacts the process of a decision and ultimately the outcome of a decision. Many studies show specifics of how the brain responds to decision-making and how the cognitive thought processes are affected as the brain coordinates a response. Some researchers believe the entire brain is involved with decision-making.

Think of all the decisions you make in a day. Imagine

the workout you give your brain constantly. What time to get up? What to eat during the day? The perceptions you coordinate in your mind about your environment, people, places, and things. Researchers have studied the impact of the information and decisions one must make and its effect on the brain. In the article "The Science of Making Decisions" Sharon Begley reports on the research of Angelika Dimoka about the impact of information overload. Dimoka's study reveals that our brain short-circuits as it becomes overloaded with information. Her study indicated that our brain shut downs and emotions rev up. "With too much information," says Dimoka, "people's decisions make less and less sense."[1] With this study, the idea that I was able to celebrate one decision while expressing "I can't believe I did that" for another decision explains the basis for the two varying results. Obviously, there are many factors in making decisions, but the concept that having information overload drastically effects decision-making explains how one decision is great and another decision may be disastrous. In many studies the ability to make decisions has been directly linked to needing an emotional component. In one case study, a patient of Antonio Damasio had part of his brain removed, which left him without emotion. Prior to surgery he had good decision-making skills. After the surgery he was unable to make the most basic decisions. The idea that women are indecisive may have been a generalization rather than the clarification that brain research explains that women may have too much information, and the brain shuts down in a response to the information overload.[2]

Women are designed to express emotion more readily than men, right? So emotional responses to "too much information" would be expressed in a heightened emotional response. Socially acceptable emotional responses drive feminine energy.

Dr. Daeyeol Lee, Yale University neurobiologist, described aspects of decision-making for the Huffington Post in 2013. When asked about people who do not evaluate their decisions and how that may impact their decisions, he expressed that loss over things or events that cannot be changed and that over-confidence in our abilities are influential in our decision-making. He responded, "Humans are all excellent decision makers. Our abilities to recall past relevant experience and to combine that with new sensory information rapidly, is truly remarkable." Decision-making is variable in the time one invests in the decision and the focus on the desired goal. Dr. Lee expressed poor decisions may have needed time to consider options and the focus of long-term or short-term goals as applicable. The evaluation of a decision, whether a good decision or a bad decision, may lie in the consideration given to the decision and the focus that is needed for a particular decision.[3]

When I was deciding on a title with my coauthors, I sent an email asking them if we should name the book *Indecisive Women*. The response I got was immediate and decisive: "Indecisive Women" was not the message or their definition for themselves.

Given the situation today with access to information available in milliseconds and the ability to get feedback from several people to hundreds of people, decision-making strategies are essential to your well-being. Designing decisions is a thought process for women to put into action as they make decisions on various levels. Among women's diversity and differences there is a common thread in our genetic make-up and our responses to our world. The differences are how we approach decisions based on what we want, our belief system, and the result or service we desire to share. Women feel free to change their decisions based on new information or experiences. Women have found freedom from the constraints of masculinity, or rules, or a belief system that doesn't serve them.

Chapter 8

Designing decisions with BARS

by Nancy Fox

"Keep your dreams alive. Understand to achieve anything requires faith and belief in yourself, vision, hard work, determination, and dedication. Remember all things are possible for those who believe." Gail Devers

BARS is an acronym for Benefits, Action, Results, and Service. I developed this concept based on humankind at its origin. From the very beginning of human life, human beings have been focused on what they want, why they want it, what action they must take to get what they want, and what happens when they get what they want. The origin of service begins with self. In order to live free and survive, humans are designed to serve themselves and to be strong and selfless with others. Service has grown over time as populations and communities have developed. This concept permeates all living organisms. One organism takes or gives as a selfless act to serve the greater good of the community.

All thoughts are based on beliefs that we can choose based on the information we receive. Many of us believe what we believe because we were taught those beliefs from generations before us. What do you believe? What is the core of your belief? Were your beliefs formed by a religious resource, because "my momma said so," an analogy of your experiences, or a random mishmash of wandering through life given a design from your experiences?

Note Gail Devers's phrase "requires faith and belief in yourself." One must start with being inside of yourself. Have you looked inward to decide what you believe and why you believe it? Today is the day that you begin or continue to explore what you believe and why you believe it.

The designing of your decisions begins with the designing of your beliefs. Yes, I said design your beliefs. You have two choices: continue with the belief system that has been designed *for* you or design your unique belief system *by* you. This is how improvement in yourself and the influence of improvement in the world begins. First, design your belief system from your experiences and the meaning you applied to those experiences and teachings, then help others look at their belief systems and help them to design belief systems based on their experiences and teachings. (Please remember when helping others you must always ask first for their permission to help them.) Scientists know that new information may change what has been believed to be true. Anyone who has trusted someone and been betrayed knows that today may show information that is believable and tomorrow can show new information that proves a change in your thinking, your beliefs. Learning is continuous if we choose to adopt thinking based on new information and the foundation of prior information. Think about your belief system in this way:

B-Benefits: What do you want your life to be for yourself and others?

A-Action: What action is needed to get what you want from your life?

R-Results: If you were closing out your life today, could you say you obtained the desires of your heart?

S-Service: Who do you serve and why do you serve them?

Work on making your life exactly as you want it to be. In what areas of your life do you want to see improvement?

Remember, today is the day you design your life. In fact, each day is the day you design your life by the daily decisions you make. Aligning the decisions with your beliefs will happen automatically based on your beliefs on any given day. If you are consciously aware of your belief system and think about how your decisions impact your plan for your life, then you will design your life instead of meandering through it. The design of your life may be changed or altered, especially the design you have right now, if you desire it to be changed.

I knew a relationship at one time that I believed was iron clad, breakup proof. The couple followed the rules that had been modeled by others (parents, grandparents, and other couples) for the relationship they wanted. I also knew each partner had the same belief system and was committed to the relationship. Friends and family knew this couple had the relationship that would last until "death do us part." As you read this description, you may know a couple like this.

This type of relationship has been described in the Bible and in the vows that couples take to commit to one another for life. These are high standards for any person who has not designed their life and their beliefs that, no matter what, they will uphold the vows of commitment to marriage. The couple was befriended by someone with a different belief system but who was pretending to have similar beliefs by attending the same church and similar social places. The person took advantage of his or her place in the couple's life and eventually committed adultery with the spouse. The couple survived the attack on their beliefs. Their love permeated their belief systems. They were both given choices/ decisions by the situation that led them to designing their lives together after weathering a massive interruption in their belief systems.

Let's be open and honest about modern life. As people have evolved opportunities for interaction with others and varying belief systems, the lack of religious standards or adherence to marriage standards or other types of rules has changed. With opportunity comes a possible change in beliefs. Changing or even violating your beliefs and what you want will impact someone or many others. Designing your life with conscious effort will make a difference on your daily decisions. Only you can decide how to design your life by using BARS for each decision throughout your life.

The stories that follow illustrate the BARS strategy. The BARS strategy is not outlined through each one, but each story reveals an understanding of how a woman reexamined her core beliefs, decided on the benefits she wanted, took action, and ultimately served herself, her loved ones, her raving fans, and certainly you, the reader of this book.

The service found between the pages of this book and beyond this book is that you, your loved ones, your friends, and anyone with whom you come in contact will get the best of you and your gifts. I challenge you to use your knowledge of BARS to see the decision-making process in each story. Connect with the stories from the women who poured their experiences onto the pages to share their challenges, their perseverance, and their triumphs. Enjoy the stories and the beauty of the women who wrote from their hearts.

part two

BARS: benefits

Chapter 9

Benefits

by Nancy Fox

"A trophy carries dust. Memories last forever."
Mary Lou Retton

Benefits are the impact you receive based on an action you take or your participation in something. A benefit is a gift, profit, or gain from someone or some action. Benefits may be a memory, a trophy or a material reward, service to others, or simply a feeling.

The first thought you probably have when embarking on a decision is: *What do I want?* or *What do I want to do?* You may not consciously be aware of this as you move towards a goal or simply decide something, but it happens many times throughout the day. When your brain asks the question, "What do I want?" it is simultaneously asking, "How will I benefit?" How you or someone else will benefit is the key question to answer when a decision is in process. I believe women intuitively ask who else will benefit. Why is this so important? This is the first step in *designing* your decisions rather than meandering through decision-making without an awareness of your desired purpose.

Explicitly or inexplicitly you choose a path for your life. The key design begins with the acknowledgment and awareness of how the decisions you make each day impact that path. If you are treading through your day, you may become aware of a place you have arrived, but the place is not your desired destiny. Have you ever asked yourself, "How did I end up here?" Then you know you were on autopilot for a period of time, and the original course you chose for your life was derailed without your awareness. Decisive women choose periods of time to be spontaneous, but usually for short periods of time or not at all. Be careful to include decisions of spontaneity. Spontaneity is essential in living your life with variety and magical moments. But be aware of the autopilot phenomenon invading your daily life that will usually leave you wondering, "How did I end up here?"

How do you design decisions with a spirit of excitement and not that of a chore? The key word here is *design*. When you are engaged in designing something it takes interest, thought, plans, and a desire for the result you visualize. You have input in the design. You have value to add to the design. You benefit.

What do you want?

Someone asked me that very question after a major situation had uprooted my beliefs, my values, my ideas of trust, and my rules. My life was upside down so I was blindsided. I was confused because my whole world was unraveling by outside forces. You may have experienced a similar situation. "What do you want?" she questioned. I could not find the words. After all, I had no structure to answer that question prior to the situation much less when all I knew was uprooted. This is when I decided to design my life, to answer the question, "What do I want?"

Many times women serve others almost from the moment they are born. Certainly many serve others when they are cognitively and physically able to do so. You may ask, "What's wrong with that?" I will never say it is wrong to serve others. Gratefully, I will say the best gifts you will ever receive are from serving others. It is in the design of serving others that you receive and satisfy the question, "What do you want?" I am saying that you need to be aware that your service is purposeful and part of your design; otherwise you may lose yourself and have underlying, opposite feelings of the purpose for serving, which is love.

Wendy Lipton-Dibner describes living your life with purpose and aligned with who you are in her book *Focus on Impact®*. Her background and business experience reveal that the creation of products and services for people and their needs is in the forefront of any endeavor that will have massive impact on the world. In her book, Wendy defines impact as "the measurable difference you make in people's lives as the direct result of contact with you, your team and your message, products and services."[1] She begins with clarity. Being clear on what you want and why you want it changes the path and the benefits you and others receive from your service.

Do you know what benefits you want for your life? You most likely have a list of things you want that you do not currently have in your possession. Benefits are not only about things, and most of us readily come up with that list.

No harm in that but let's look at other benefits that may be among your desires.

Benefits may be tangible/physical, emotional, and spiritual. The ones we often think about are physical/tangible. The things we can hold, touch, and see, such as a new dress, a new pair of shoes, a new car, a new home, a new electronic device, a new (your choice of benefit). The emotional benefits are connections with others, a relationship, a birth of a son or daughter or relative, a wedding, a beautiful sunrise or sunset, and many events, situations, or just being that evoke emotion. In fact, we dance through emotions throughout our days and our lives. The spiritual benefits may be a connection with self, your creator, the people who have passed, or a religious belief. Benefits surround us and envelop us throughout our day. We have choices to feel, do, and see tremendous particles of our lives that we filter through and sift out the design of our lives.

An example of seeking a benefit is the story of Adele's song "Hello." The chorus exclaims the forgiveness and the healing she is seeking. She describes wanting to get in touch with someone to talk about an event that changed their paths in life and left them out of touch with one another.

The struggle within herself about an ex-lover, friend, or family member surely is the story at first glance. If you look at this from the perspective of forgiveness and healing, you can give yourself forgiveness for the decisions that you have made and the healing you may need from making those decisions. Ladies, we can be our worst enemies. The first benefit to seek is to forgive yourself and look toward the benefits that serve you in amazing ways. Begin today to love yourself right where you are; accept all that you have learned thus far from your beliefs, your decisions, your choice of benefits; and begin the design of your life.

To find the physical, emotional, and spiritual benefits you are seeking is a significant key to the design of your life. These benefits are with you, as demonstrated in the stories that follow. The women who tell these stories show that designing your decisions promotes a journey, a path, and a life. The relationships that you develop with others will have an impact on the journey you pursue. In fact, living life must have relationships of all varieties in order to live life to the fullest with love, one of our basic needs. Many times we hide the desires of our heart because of past experiences, or we are spending time pleasing others. The journey begins with us each day.

- What do you want? How will you benefit? Who will benefit?
- Take some time to reach into your soul and find the truth about what you want. How do you want to feel? Explore your childhood dreams. Experience the things that make you happy and you describe as fun. How will you benefit? Who will benefit?
- Think of all the possibilities that your presence can impact someone's life.

Chapter 10

The lion inside

by Sandra Champlain

There are moments in life that you are never prepared for. Many are in times of crisis. Depending on who you are and what you've experienced, the "fight or flight" response that lives within you will cause you to react to certain situations. One time you might see a person needing your help and without a thought you are there to give aid. Other times for whatever reason and with no logic, you might flee.

I have always found myself as one who doesn't fight. It is my usual behavior to either "take flight" or try to soothe or mend a situation. Does my behavior come from my past? I grew up as the middle child, the peacekeeper and the people pleaser. I never believed I was special. My parents had their hands full with three kids in diapers at the same time, as my twin siblings are just a year older than me. To stand out, I became the sweet, loving, generous, quiet, and "never-a-problem" Sandra.

This pattern continued for forty-four years. Did I have what I wanted in life? No. Did I have a lot of frustration? Definitely. Did I respect people who said what was on their minds no matter what hot water they found themselves in? Absolutely! I never had the courage to stand up for my wants, and I was always fearful of negative consequences, such as being called selfish. I guess the word I would use to describe myself would be "wimp." I knew that I would never be one of those people who had a backbone.

My life was turned upside down during the first months of 2010. My father had a cancerous tumor break apart his spine. Dad was a twenty-mile-a-day bicycle rider, in great shape even in his seventies. Although the tumor was radiated, it left Dad with incredible pain, being connected to an intravenous pain medicine pump and wearing a hard, protective "turtle shell" around his torso to prevent further injury. To make matters worse, blood tests showed that cancer remained in his body and couldn't be treated because his system was weak and there was no visual sign of cancer on CT scans.

As with many families in crisis, my siblings and I had to make decisions about our father's care. What was predictable was that I, the people pleaser, would sit quietly and let my siblings make the decisions. However, some powerful force seemed to arise from me, one that I never saw coming.

I can only imagine it was a protective, survival instinct similar to a mother doing whatever possible to protect her child. I envision a lioness doing whatever needed to protect her young cubs from danger.

The final months of Dad's life certainly brought the lion out in me. I became the patient advocate, looking out for my father's best interests. In the hospital, I was by his side as much as I could be, often from the time he woke up in the morning to the time he fell asleep at night. I would call upon the nursing staff when needed and was actively involved in the doctor's visits. Dad was clear with me what he wanted and didn't want. I did all I knew to do, gave all I had to give, and even got as creative to find ways to bring joy into his hospital room.

I was not the only lion in the family. I have three siblings that also loved my extraordinary father. They had children of their own and family responsibilities where I did not, so I spent more time with Dad than anyone. Sometimes there are family arguments leading to siblings no longer speaking as a result of a parent's death. That was the last thing I would have predicted in my family, as I have extremely smart, loving, and compassionate siblings.

However disagreements began happening, and miscommunications became common. Intertwined in days filled with fear, uncertainty, and love for my father, arguments became painfully common.

My micro-decision came when my brother asked me a question. In a split second it was one of those "life flashing before my eyes" events that we often hear about. My future life seemed to flash in front of me. I could see only two options: One path was to tell my brother my truth and stand my ground, which would very probably have my siblings disown me. The second path was to lie and play it safe, safeguarding our relationship even though I would have let myself down in the process. Without warning, the wimp disappeared and the lioness appeared. I was honest. I stood my ground. I decided to take the path of being true to myself.

What followed was the darkest time of my life. On May 11, 2010, I watched as my wonderful father took his last breaths on Earth. In addition, my three siblings believed a story about me that was simply untrue, and I lost relationships with them. The grief I felt from losing my father was so painful, and the grief I felt from losing my siblings as well was horrendous. I would never wish that pain on anyone.

I have heard it said that within the word *decide* is the Latin word *cide*. Cide means "to cut, to strike, or to kill." The words *suicide, homicide*, and even *spermicide* all mean that something is killed off. When we "decide," do we kill something off? I think so. With my father, I decided to pick one path and kill off the other. That doesn't sound very powerful though, does it?

We can each live however we want, that is the beauty of free will. One can be a victim in life, or one can have power and declare oneself responsible for one's actions and the results. I can honestly tell you that I lived for a while as a victim after Dad died. Sad, depressed, and miserable, it was so easy to tell my story and make all the others in my life wrong.

However, one day a new thought came to my mind. What if, instead of deciding what path to take, I actually chose to be powerful and speak my mind? What if this situation was put before me so that I might know that I really am strong and courageous, and I have a backbone to stick up for my beliefs? What if this situation was in my life to provide some knowledge to me and perhaps make a difference for others and myself?

I feel that I made another micro-decision or, better yet, a choice in that moment. I was no longer going to be a victim of my circumstances and ride in the backseat of my very own life. Instead, I took responsibility for my actions and jumped right up front behind the wheel in the driver's seat!

I channeled all the energy my grief brought me into

research. I found out that almost 50 percent of sibling relationships end when a parent dies. I found that 80 percent of couples get divorced after a child dies. There were other figures, as well, of relationships that end after a loss of a job, loss of health, or when an adult child leaves the house, as with the empty nest. My power came back! No longer was I a victim, but now I was on a crusade to discover why this happens. I found that in every example above, grief is present.

As I began to research the world of grief, I discovered what happens chemically in our fragile heads when any kind of a loss occurs. One of the biggest things I learned was how memory, communication, and perception areas in the brain become faulty as we grieve. We often hear about the feel-good endorphins released after we have exercised or laughed. However, when grief occurs, a feeling of loss is triggered in our brains, and then anger, sadness, memory loss, and other side effects arise. In a split second I saw how my siblings and I were fighting about things that were not based in truth. I am not certain they understood what I was trying to communicate based on Dad's wishes, and I am certain that I could not see the situation from their shoes either. Who was to blame? No one, it was simply a by-product of grief.

As a victim, I believed that the time surrounding my dad's death was the worst thing that ever happened to me. Now, being in the driver's seat, I choose to believe it was the best thing that has ever happened to me. Is that the truth? Only I can say that it is my truth. I am now a warrior to help people understand that when a loss occurs the grieving mind is compassionate with those in your life and mends relationships.

After Dad passed away I recorded "How to Survive Grief," a free audio that has been downloaded tens of thousands of times around the world on a website I created called "survive grief." Courageously, I choose to share my other passion, investigating the world of life after death. I combined life after death, grief, and my ultimate message of "how to have a powerful life" and published the book *We Don't Die—A Skeptic's Discovery of Life after Death,* which has become a #1 international bestseller in the United States, Canada, and the United Kingdom. A documentary has been made about me; there are numerous radio programs, television interviews, and speeches of me speaking about grief on the Internet; and now I am the host of my own radio show. I will never stop sharing my message and empowering people to understand grief and live powerful lives.

Life can bring much joy but it can also bring much pain. I ask that you be compassionate with yourself and don't be so hard on yourself. Every day in life we have choices to make; trust that you have always made the right choices. Use every experience to learn and to grow, and more importantly, use your life lessons to help a fellow traveler on his or her path. I certainly don't have all the answers, but I do know that there is much more peace living in the driver's seat than being a passenger!

Chapter 11

I choose life

by Denver Beaulieu-Hains

I was suffocating. I was drowning in a pool of cold, frothy liquid. The air was chasing me, and I couldn't catch it. Everything was moving in slow motion. I was frozen in time, wondering how I'd gotten there in the first place, and for the second time . . . then there was a short pause as the first bottle was empty, while he proceeded to open the next. He poured that one, too, over my head. Down my face it ran. Again, the bubbly foam left the bottle, sizzling and puckering on my skin. Then it began all over again, rhythmic waves of pungent ale. It danced over my head and into my nostrils. I gasped for air and fought the stream only for it to end in a disbelief that carried me to the kitchen for the brand new pack of kitchen knives. He ransacked my new apartment, looking for clues of a new man or some telltale sign of infidelity that would have made me want to leave and to move out. The irony is that he never saw his behavior as a contributing factor.

Following the heated exchange, as he continued to violate my privacy and privilege, I found the pointy end of a knife desirable. I envisioned myself making him go. Threatening to do him harm and winning; I wanted to make him leave. I also wanted to ensure this would never happen again. However, I was only brought to reality by the sound of my daughter's voice. It was an echo at first, "Mommy, please put the knife away," she cried. Next, it came a little louder, "Mommy, put the knife away. He'll kill you!" And, as I came to my senses, I heard her plea a little louder "If you don't put the knife away, he will kill you," she said more urgently this time. Then, I heard, "Who'll take care of us?"

That thought stopped me in my tracks. I emerged from my trance. Her sweet, innocent voice reminded me I was all they had. I knew I was important to them, but in my own lack of self-esteem, it escaped me that without me my children may suffer. For me, this sacred moment was the equivalent of hearing God's voice—her voice, a premonition of what was to come if I didn't stop and take stock of my choices and myself. I knew deep down that I was important, and that I needed to live. It wasn't my time. I heard God, loud and clear. This could be my end if I didn't take control of myself.

In this instance, I gave myself permission to give in; it was okay to surrender to the moment because there would be another day. I'd have another chance at life. This was all that mattered. No manner of force would beat the physical strength of my husband. I knew that, and I opened the drawer, placed the open knife into its original packaging. I closed the drawer and waited.

A terrible situation was stalled and I'd been spared. My angels were watching over me. There was no escalation; instead I was restored by the peace of knowing that I'd live another day and that my choices were powerful. For the first time, I recognized my influence over all the situations in my life.

I wasn't a victim. I was never a victim. That day, I took charge of myself, became mindful and powerful. Later, my vengeance was my ability to be self-sufficient and successful. Eighty ounces of malt liquor, a man, and a new perspective on life caused a shift in my behavior that set me up for the future. I was very aware that I'd made the mess of my life, and I knew I was the only one that could fix it. This was a fact drawn from many years of complication, worry, and self-doubt. I'd waited for my savior to come, but I was stuck. There was no man on a white horse, only me. By the time I recognized my crazy, I thought it was too late.

In 1990, I'd graduated from college. During commencement, I walked across the stage eight months pregnant. My decision not to return home landed me a marriage shortly thereafter. I felt I'd disappointed my family because I was pregnant, and I didn't want to face them. I had a lot of pride, and despite knowing I was probably making a bad decision, I had to do it my way. I committed. I moved in with him and his family. His family members are good people, and they loved and embraced me as part of their clan. I am forever indebted in particular to his mother. As I began to branch out and begin my own career, she never denied my children a place to stay. To this day, I'm her daughter. However, back then I'm sure I needed counseling. I tried a long time ago, but I cried a lot and it hurt. So, I'd stop going and pretend everything was okay.

Some of my difficulties in marriage likely stem from my own dysfunctions at home when I was growing up, and witnessing my parents' failed marriage and domestic abuse.

As a preteen, I remember eating pancakes for dinner because there was nothing else to eat, and staying in a dark house with no heat and water. Those experiences conditioned me to pretend that everything was okay, no matter what. I was told I couldn't talk about those things. My grandparents would never have tolerated it. But being the oldest, I couldn't tell them about it without shaming my mother.

Even now, after all these years, I report it in disbelief and fear because it is among my family's deepest, darkest secrets. No one would have ever guessed. But I can't live in the shadow of my past. I want a new future for my children and my grandchildren as I begin to look ahead. However, it was a big deal when the bulb went off and I got it. I'm somebody! I can't live like this!

The difference for me was the fear in my children's faces and the deep conversations we would have. "Mommy, you should have a husband who loves you," said my oldest daughter with concern in her voice. I felt like a fool, "Why don't I know that already?" I thought.

I later became a journalist in the Army, and I've researched stories on domestic violence and abuse. I've learned that there are difficulties in prosecuting cases sometimes because victims don't always respond to abuse the way judges and juries expect. I stayed and tolerated it for about eight years because I didn't recognize it as abuse right away. I had grown used to such a high degree of crazy that I'd developed a tolerance even for insanely crazy. Literally, it took an act of God to shock me into a healthy place.

When I sought help, my steps were deliberate and systematic.

First, my husband and I started marriage counseling, but I always felt like the two of them, my husband and his doctor, were conspiring against me. I felt like I was the problem after an hour-long session. So I found my own doctor, someone I thought would advocate for me. In my individual counseling I don't remember what we talked about, but I understood for the first time that I had rights. I also knew what to do after a violent incident. This was critical to me.

Second, I'd made the decision to begin to document the events. I did this because I'd be confused about the events. He'd say, "If you hadn't done this, then that wouldn't have happened." After a while I was confused everything was my fault. I'd hurt him and he was just responding to me.

I only went to the hospital once. When I was doused that day, I decided I'd had enough. That was the beginning of the rest of my life. Again though, God stepped in. Life is also very much about timing. It seems that I'd made my decision to leave, but things weren't in order or aligned for me at the time. Once again, the universe intervened, finally, after a long day at the hospital.

I returned to my small, first floor apartment to use the phone. I couldn't find my handbag. It was missing in all the confusion. As I dialed, a rat the size of a small dog slid from under the door of the utility room. It was surprisingly tall and grossly swollen. I was shocked the rat could fit through the small opening under the door, but it did. The smell of beer brought him out from hiding. He was there to challenge me, but I didn't have any fight left that day. I saw him. It was a no contest fight. I left that night never to return. My next steps shocked even me. I drove across town to my husband. He took me back, and I stayed for another couple of years. We, my husband and I, had successfully completed another cycle of abuse. This observation only was realized after seeking counseling. It was certainly confirmation that I was on the right track, but I still had a long way to go.

Tensions build, incident, reconciliation, and calm are the characteristics coined by Lenore E. Walker in her social cycle theory. I'd officially recognized myself and, more importantly, my role in the process. Sometimes when you live in dysfunction for a long time, you don't recognize it because it becomes your norm. The veil of secrecy kept my pain, confusion, and dysfunction hidden from everyone around me, including myself. I'd lived life thinking everyone lived this way. It was all I knew. My mother and father hadn't provided the best example. Neither my husband nor I grew up in homes with two parents. We were living, breathing examples of dysfunction.

Despite my fear that night, I'm thankful for the rat, which I believe died in my place that day. During a synchronistic moment in time we met, the rat in its final hour and I at a critical, pivotal starting point in my life. The rat was sick. Earlier in the week, I'd complained to the apartment complex staff about strange noises in the night. They found a hole between my apartment and the adjoining tenant. The hole was sealed and the poison was left as a precaution. It was the luck of the draw the rat was sealed into my apartment that night. He was likely hungry, thirsty, and fatigued, just like me. I lived and he didn't. He was looking for food and water. The beer sprayed around the apartment was his last ditch effort at life. Since I believe everything has a purpose, his was to move me toward my destiny, and he did. I grasped my faith in a way I'd never known. The rat, symbolized God. The circumstance became my personal mountain. My spiritual self took control, and I learned to push the rational self away, at least temporarily so I could begin again. I wanted a better life for my kids. I needed God; I didn't have enough courage in myself at the time to do it on my own. I'd created negative labels and self talk that would have destroyed me had I allowed anything besides the unconditional love of the divine to steer me toward the future. My faith averted my feelings of inadequacy, vulnerability, and contempt. At the time, I berated myself for showing weakness and indecisiveness. I was ashamed and confused, but I'd resorted to a supernatural understanding of the events, which ultimately saved me.

Disappointment, like guilt and shame, can prevent one from moving forward. I was hurt that my attempt at independence was a flop. And additionally, a consequence of the failed attempt was a sense of increased alienation from my family, which is another classic symptom of abuse. However, a single focus and a dogged resolve meant that circumstance didn't stop me from trying again. After that, I focused on small achievements and applauded myself when I had minimal successes. This was important to my healing because abusers may capitalize on failures and shortcomings to validate a victim's lack of security, love, and support, which allows a victim to feel powerless.

I felt at times that I had nowhere to go. I continued to push forward for the next window of opportunity, which came when I traded my dependent ID card for a military ID card. I became a soldier shortly thereafter. I always believed that God would provide me a safe place, and I knew I owed it to myself to plan for that day. No one would ever douse me with any liquid again. When I showed up at the military hospital in South Korea, my doctor said, “I don’t ever have to worry about you again. No matter what, you’ll be okay,” he said.

I’d reported for duty, and he had the opportunity to see me all shined up in my military uniform. I was a product of his careful prodding and support. I didn’t know it at the time, but I was better than okay.

Chapter 12

The best tool in the box

by Dianne Burch

The greatest obstacle to decision-making is usually fear. We are afraid of what will change and often decide to endure the known difficulties rather than risk the unknown possibilities. I chose to remain in a bad marriage for more than eighteen years, in part due to fear of change. Oddly enough, the key that later freed me from this situation was handed to me by my husband in the first year of our marriage.

Fear is commonly based in irrational thinking. This fact became crystal clear to me many years ago in the first six months of my marriage. Like most couples starting out, we had more debt than assets as we began to build our life together. In our case, he had long-term steady employment and great benefits with a major company. I had a solid job with great income but long hours of nights and weekends, leaving little time with my new husband. We made the decision that I should seek other employment, and I began training with a respected company, but the pay was straight commission. We had a land payment, mobile home payment, one car payment, and one fully paid-off, pieced-together old Jeep. With his salary and benefits, we could meet the bills and get by until I built up my customer base and began producing income again. Life was good.

Then one evening, only three months after I'd started training in my new job, my husband surprised me with news that he was ready to quit his job. He needed to borrow five thousand dollars for a down payment on a small company he wanted to buy. He spent all of fifteen minutes explaining why it would be great and how much he *thought* he would be able to make, including the monthly payments for the first three years of the business. I f-r-e-a-k-e-d out! All I could hear was he wanted to quit his job, the only salary and benefits that we had, and that he would be adding to our already barely-squeaking-by debt load. I began expressing all my logical objections and asking questions. He was never one for lengthy conversation. After all, he'd invested fifteen minutes telling me everything I needed to know. He wondered what more he could say or needed to be said. In his mind—"No brainer." In my mind—"Are you crazy?"

As my questions kept coming, his frustration reached its limits, and he fired off in anger the best question, the best statement, he ever made to me: "What are you so afraid of? My God, woman, they can't take our skin!" It was brilliantly stupid. It shut me up fast trying to make sense of what he said. Then it made me laugh. When I thought about it, I realized how irrational my fears were. We were young, healthy, intelligent, capable people. Here was a man expressing his dream and a not too bad plan to pursue it. Here was a woman reacting as if the entire world would stop revolving if this failed to be successful. Yes, it could affect our credit. We might possibly lose things we did not yet own. No, we would not be homeless. We had people who loved us and would, at the very least, let us sleep in their garage and offer us bread and water. We would likely still be employable and might have to start again. Then of course, there was the possibility it might succeed and grow and be the best decision we ever made.

The bluntness of his remark stopped my crazy mind. First, I was shocked he yelled at me, and second, I had to process that odd phrase: "They can't take our skin." That single phrase has never left me. In that moment I learned one of the most valuable lessons ever. Without realizing it, he had given me a tool that I have used repeatedly to assess the true risk behind every major decision I have made since that night.

Most decisions we face throughout life do not involve life or death consequences, yet we often react as if they do. That is fear, and our minds can be masterful at creating imagined threats. Now I clear away the nonsense, the irrational, fear-based junk that tries to stop me from encountering opportunity. Once you know whether or not you are actually risking your "skin," the decisions come much easier.

That simple little statement is truthfully the best thing I took from a nearly eighteen-year marriage. The business was successful. We built it together, we grew it together, and we ultimately found it was the only common basis of our relationship. Yet that simple little statement helped create a very strong woman. I even used it when deciding to end the marriage, because remaining there in all its emptiness was taking my skin and all that was contained within it.

It helped me make the decision to finally invest my time, energy, and resources in my own dream. I used that tool to decide to end a marriage, close two businesses, and take three years to stop everything and be caregiver for my mother until her death. And finally, I was able to pursue my passion of being an advocate for animal welfare shelters and rescues.

With that stupidly brilliant phrase as a point of reference, I have been able to take real risks, look at them objectively, and weigh the possible gains against the possible losses. Fear no longer has the power to stop me from dreaming my dreams and taking the steps to make them reality. I am often amazed at the risks I have found the courage to take, and even more amazed at the opportunities that have been made possible because of it.

When I ended my marriage, I thought that would be the hard part, and I was prepared to figure out the rest—confident I could at least keep my skin intact. However, life often has its own plans and the toughest parts were still to be. My ex-husband was remarried to a former friend before he even had our final divorce papers. Then my brother abruptly closed the business I'd been helping him to build. I bravely used my measuring phrase and mustered the courage to keep the lease on our building and continue with my own business plan. Just a few short months into the venture, my sister's husband died suddenly, her son was critically injured, and our mother's health began a rapid decline, requiring full-time care. I was the one most able to shut down my own plans and be there for everyone else.

That period of caring for family lasted for nearly five years. When all the storylines came to a close, I was left to pick up the pieces of my own life and figure out how to start everything over. My trusty phrase got lots of use.

The first test was allowing myself to dream again. I'd not thought of what I wanted, what was important to me, or what I was good at for many, many years. I dared to let myself play with the possibilities of all the things that would make me the happiest. I knew I needed to update my marketing skills since billboards and direct mail were not as popular as they had once been. During the previous five years, I'd survived off what should have been retirement assets. There had also been some significant cash outlays for numerous emergency repairs at my home. Money was a huge focus, and I needed to be creating an income, not spending what little was left. I knew I would have to invest in myself for the first time ever in my life. I really needed that little phrase then. I could not believe how hard it was to have the same belief in myself and my abilities that I so fervently supported in everyone else. My handy little tool allowed me to take that leap of faith for myself. I invested in training to learn about writing and publishing. I had challenges and fear every step of the way, but I never once found anything that threatened my skin, so I pushed on.

Less than two years later, that powerful, all-assessing phrase had helped me measure my way to writing and publishing a children's book together with a new love interest. We encouraged each other to be bold and reach for a life that would be fulfilling. Animals have always been my "children," and my passion has been a deep desire to help people understand the importance animals hold in our human lives. I've wanted to help stray and shelter animals for all my adult life. Now with the children's book, I am able to be a voice for animals in need, and I help bring a positive light to rescue and shelter pets. I visit schools and other groups to share the book and its "Mutts on a Mission" message with families, children, and people of all ages. I speak to groups about the amazing human-animal bond as well as the journey of reinventing your world when life cleans your slate.

Many times in this journey, I have felt that level of fear that tries to stop you cold—the dream-crushing, opportunity-stealing fear that makes you tell yourself total untruths. Every time I felt it, I took a long, deep breath, and I measured the real possibilities of the outcome. Although the fear would have me believe it, there was not one time that my skin was ever in danger. Everything else seemed manageable and the possibilities . . . look very bright!

Chapter 13

Junior

by Natalie H. G. London

Some sidekicks are just inevitable. Every good lead has one; every great adventure begins with one—Batman and Robin, Lucy and Ethel, Watson and Holmes. I grew up with philosophically-thick childhood movies, the kind that impress the importance of the untamed and supernatural sidekick—the *NeverEnding Story's* Atreyu and his giant luck dragon, Sarah from *Labyrinth* with Ludo the gentle beast, Max and the *Where the Wild Things Are.*

The most important decisions I've ever made are based on instinct, based on that innate gut reaction that leads you to what you need, regardless of whether or not your mind can completely comprehend it. Sometimes it leads you to decisions that appear outright ridiculous; sometimes they appear completely illogical! But that decision-making process, if you really listen, doesn't take long at all. It doesn't even take five minutes.

I can't remember exactly how I ended up in a remote part of Ramona, California. I know I was visiting my mom on a break from my senior year at Columbia University. I had arrived exhausted and worn-out. I know it was spring.

The year up to that point had been one of the most terrorizing of my life, an erratic blur of confusion. I had been tossed around from hospital to hospital, misdiagnosed by every doctor I'd seen.

I was formerly a straight-A student, a go-getter, a working three jobs "do anything I have to do to get where I want to go" kind of girl. I was quickly on my way to becoming a *formerly* successful musician while record label meetings waited unanswered for me across the country. I was a formerly focused scholar, a formerly active member of the world.

By the time I ended up in San Diego that spring, you could have added "Former" to my name itself and it would have been accurate.

I sat in the passenger's seat of my mom's dusty 4Runner, hugging the turns of the hot southern California mountains. I was too tired to really care where we were going. She pulled into a long dirt driveway and up towards a farm. Approaching the car was the largest dog I'd ever seen.

"I think you need to play with some puppies, maybe think about getting one someday," my mom clued me into the reason for the trip.

She had trained therapy dogs for years, and as far as she knew, all my ailments were results of a sudden depression everyone incorrectly believed I was suffering from, so perhaps a pet could help.

We were welcomed into an area with about ten rescues and twenty puppies. My mom pushed me through the gate, nudging me to go pet them.

I sat down in the middle of the dry dirt baking in the mid-afternoon sun, and I watched and waited. Curious puppies chased each other and fell over me but within minutes the pack dissipated—leaving one tiny thoughtful puppy across from me, staring.

Many great decisions are nothing more than a response to life handing you a perfect moment. If you can truly be present in those moments you'll find that the decision you must make is really just a choice between two things: accept the opportunity in front of you or turn it away.

Sitting there in the dirt my decision was made.

"I found him," I said concisely as the one wistful puppy walked up and sat in my lap.

"What do you mean?" my mom asked. "I just wanted you to think about getting a dog someday."

"No, this is he. We can go."

I signed the paperwork and spent almost the last of my money. As I held him on my lap while my mom drove, I'll be honest with you, my brain was wondering what in f-ing hell I was doing at that moment. He was this giant white fur ball with paws. It looked like I stole him from Antarctica. There was no logical reason for me to take this baby polar bear back to my habitat. But that is the great thing about quick decisions . . . the logic behind that gut response—the whys—will absolutely come later. In this case those whys were more than I could have ever imagined.

I had to name my new friend something sarcastic, so I chose to call him Junior. It was either going to be that or Tiny.

I'm not sure if you've ever seen a white Great Pyrenees, but if so you may very well have crossed to the other side of the street. They are one of the few giant breeds, weighing up to a massive two hundred pounds. Standing on their hind legs, they are taller than the average man.

I couldn't fly back to New York with my new puppy, and so arrived Junior and my first adventure.

I convinced my friend Scott to hop into my 1983 Delta 88 Oldsmobile and drive three thousand miles across the country with me. At only twelve weeks old and already forty pounds, Junior and I slept in the back on the couch-like bench seats, breathing in the untainted air through the four open windows. I taught him how to drink from a water bottle as we made our way across the scorching deserts of the southwest. We crashed on the floor with an old love in his rundown home in Austin, Texas; we explored Lafayette Square and wandered around New Orleans at sunrise. We found ourselves in the forests of Georgia, and days later finally reached the George Washington Bridge as we crossed back over into Harlem.

I didn't last long back at school. By late spring I was so sick I was unable to remember how to do almost anything. I could no longer even read or write.

The previous summer my band was visiting Charlottesville, Virginia. I had been bit by a tick but thought nothing much of it. Unknown to all those around me, I was fighting a life-threatening case of Lyme disease as well as multiple co-infections. All year I had suffered from pain and insomnia, minor seizures, breathing restrictions, and a slew of other symptoms. I finally knew I couldn't fight on my own anymore. I packed up my belongings, dropped out, and found two strangers looking for a ride to help take Junior and me back to California where I was immediately hospitalized in the infectious disease ward.

It took a year and a half to diagnose me. I spent a total of approximately three years bedridden, unable for months at a time to walk or talk. I lived in a ten- by ten-foot room where I had a total of four PICC lines to my heart, took hundreds of pills, plus daily infusions of antibiotics and antiviral through my IVs.

You'd think that it was the three years while I was sickest that Junior played the most important role to me. As so many who have suffered from a very serious or life-threatening illness know, you find out very fast who your friends are. Too many people disappear, and my case was heartbreakingly no different. It is true that the unconditional love I got from Junior helped ease the losses and the loneliness now and then; there was a true comfort to the quiet companionship, the loyalty. But that's not why seizing the opportunity to take Junior home with me that day in Ramona was one of the best decisions of my life.

What most people don't realize is coming out of an illness can be as terrifying as being in it. I had lived in extraordinary isolation. I had lost almost everything and everyone I defined my life by, and I had felt death's breath linger a little too long against my face. Reemerging into the world was not simple by any means.

While I was ill, Junior was trained and certified to become a service animal. At 185 pounds and now coming up to my waist, Junior was trained to help me learn how to walk again. He could hold me up to counteract my vertigo, get me up stairs, and wake me up from nightmares. I had severe PTSD from being conscious while nearly bleeding out after my artery was nicked during a hospital procedure gone wrong. He howled to alert me if I was reliving that moment in my sleep or if I was in a crowd and nearing a seizure or serious chest pains. He guarded me day and night, sensing and pacifying every moment of panic and pain.

I was committed to going back to Columbia University to finish that final semester when I was forced to drop out. To go from complete seclusion to the most crowded city in the country was a surreal change of scenery to say the least. Together, Junior and I flew in the plane, took the subways, busses, and cabs. With my giant headphones always like a soundtrack to my comeback, Junior and I made our way through the world. It was me and my polar bear . . . in classes, on the street, in the library . . . my giant always next to me, backing up my every move.

After years of solitude it was difficult to remember how to speak to people, but Junior broke the ice everywhere we'd go. From the toughest man to the most arrogant woman, *everyone* dropped his or her guard around Junior. Nobody could keep from smiling. He appeared to enter campus with me from another world. He subconsciously connected those we came across with the childhood version of them, that part of us that remembers the joy of true imagination and mystery and adventure. Not a day went by where someone didn't run up to me yelling "It's the luck dragon!" or "Fantasia!" or "Narnia!"

Illness had stripped away everything I had been and built up—every day of pain and loneliness, seclusion and sickness, chipped away and chipped away until all that was left was the most basic version of myself. I felt fresh to the world again. I felt reborn, like a child. And as I said from the start, every childhood adventurer going out into the world needs a confidant, a protector, and a fellow explorer. Every child-hearted human being needs a sidekick.

As I regained my strength, Junior continued to reconnect me with core instincts and the ferocity of simple joys. We wrestled and we brawled, my arms always covered in bruises and teeth marks from play-fighting with my bear. We trekked our way through the rare silence of snow-covered city grounds at night, running through blizzards, falling down. We covered thousands and thousands of miles on the road where we had truly first met one another, the road that will always be our second home. We swam out into lakes. We tackled waves in the sea. We explored cities we'd never seen. From fancy nights walking red carpets in Los Angeles with Junior, as I eventually reconnected with the music/entertainment world again, to living on a ranch with hundreds of horses. Nowhere was off limits. No fear. No need to be.

In that moment, years earlier, I made the decision to seize the opportunity, to welcome what appeared illogical. I made the decision because somewhere deep inside me I believed that one day I would find freedom again and when that day came, I would need the perfect sidekick to embrace the world with. I'd need the perfect sidekick to remember that it always has been, and always will be, our world for the taking.

Chapter 14

Brotherly love

by Virginia Rector

Have you ever experienced the death of a sibling? I have, and putting what it feels like into words is difficult. I felt empty. Emptiness to me has no sound. I felt like I existed, but could not interact within my contexts. My day-to-day activities were surreal. I felt blank; I felt numb. In the movie *Deja Vu*, Denzel Washington goes back in time to prevent a domestic terror attack as well as prevent the death of a loved one. In comparison, if I could, I would have prevented the death of my brother.

I am from a small family. We lived in a rental house at 156 Washington Street. The community was a mixture of low- to middle-income families. At the least, our neighbors all knew each other by our last names. The municipal population is now about 37,000. In our city there were certain Baptist churches, known as the "big four," attended by mostly African Americans; our street was located behind one of the churches. During that time, it was prestigious to attend one of the big four. We were a Christian family that together had scripture and prayer before eating breakfast every Sunday morning. I have one sister named Barbara, referred to as Barbara Jean by my mom and dad, and another sister named Barbara by her mother—we had the same father. Although my siblings were reared together, I love my brothers and sisters. Barbara Jean and I attended a Pentecostal church with my mother; however, my brother Gary Jr. and father attended the Baptist church. Each summer my sister and I, as most of the neighborhood children, attended vacation Bible school at my father's church. It was fun to play and meet new friends, as well as eat the delicious refreshments that were served each day. As a family, we also enjoyed music and singing; we were a happy, loving family.

Gary Jr. was my only brother. He was my mother's first born. There was ten years difference in our ages. Everything that Gary, Jr. and Barbara Jean did growing up seemed to be a lot more fun than when I came along. I used to enjoy looking at old pictures of him and Barbara Jean dressed up in their cowboy and cowgirl outfits. I also enjoyed listening to stories about how Barbara Jean always thought that she was supposed to jump into every fight Gary Jr. was ever involved in.

Our parents died in 1994 and 1996. After their deaths, my brother became the patriarch of the family. The stories my mother told us about my brother's childhood always left the impression that he was her pride and joy. She shared that she used to enjoy dressing him up in some of the finest clothes that were in style during his childhood. I never got the impression that he was reared under the strict upbringing as Barbara Jean and me. As a teenager, he and his friends always had the best times. I can recall Gary Jr. and some of his buddies learning to make electronic speakers in his old high school's shop class. At that time, making loudspeakers in shop was just as common as making small remote-controlled drones in today's tech class. The joy that he and his friends had among themselves spread because it was exuberant across communities. Before the Internet, cell phones, texting, and Facebook, aside from the Civil Rights Movement, the Vietnam War and protests, the 60s represented an era of young teens that communicated day-to-day, face-to-face, or by using a local area network (LAN) telephone. They enjoyed their high school years. One summer, my brother and a few friends decided to wire and set the speakers in trees to amplify rock and roll music at a community block party that teens from surrounding neighborhoods attended. Even adults dropped by to observe them having fun, and on occasion, demonstrated to the teens what real dancing was like. Gary, Jr. and his classmates always seemed to enjoy living life to the fullest, and they had the support of the adults who lived in the community.

Just before the Christmas holiday, the high school bands always marched in the Christmas parade. With Gary Jr. performing in the tenor saxophone section, it was exciting to wait in anticipation for the Carver High School band to march downtown. The sound, the cadence, and the sight of the garnet and grey band suits always moved the crowds to explosive cheers. Also, while in high school, Gary Jr. decided to join a couple of R&B local bands that played in small nightclubs. Since we had a love for music and came from a musically endowed family, our parents often offered our home as a safe haven for the band to rehearse. Gary once told us that one of the bands he played with was the opening act for James Brown. This was big news, and we didn't hesitate to tell everybody. After graduating high school he left home to live with relatives in California and attend college, but he was drafted in 1968 into the United States Army. Soon, thereafter, he was deployed to Vietnam. My mother was so distraught that she sent to him recordings of her voice with messages of hope and encouragement. On one occasion, she also sent to him and his unit fried chicken and biscuits. Upon receipt, my brother declared that the chicken tasted as if it was just cooked; we never knew for certain if he ate it. I can only imagine the pain my mother felt over her only son being sent away to fight on foreign soil.

When Gary Jr. returned home, he married his high school sweetheart and together they reared three young men. Again, joy was brought to the family with us sharing in the love and nurturing of three sons: Gary III, Kenneth, and Anthony. Some years later, life took a different turn, and Gary Jr. began to develop some problems with his health. We're not certain, but while in Vietnam, he may have been exposed to Agent Orange, a toxic defoliant herbicide mixture that was sprayed to destroy the forest. There could have been something else that affected his health; regardless, his condition worsened and led to an aneurysm. Gary Jr. lived five years with some minor complications and many doctor visits. His sixtieth birthday was in June 2004. I remember a few months later, just after Christmas, he said to me, "I was happy to see sixty; I never thought I would live to see it." I embraced his words, but didn't realize that would be my last time seeing him alive. My son and I would be traveling to Delaware the next morning to attend my husband's installation service. Gary Jr. died before his sixty-first birthday. I came to the epiphany that some people are ashamed of getting older and often take life for granted.

My mind fast-forwarded, and I realized that the very next year I would become sixty; I hoped to live to see it.

The death of my brother caused a great abyss in our hearts. He had kept alive the musical talents that were passed along through the generations on our father's side of the family. He had been a talented musician. He loved various genres of music, but his favorite was R&B, soul and gospel. My heart sank because I never gave him his Christmas gift, a cassette tape with favorite hits by Ray Charles. I felt that a great void was created by the absence of my brother. There were so many unanswered questions. Why did he die at sixty? Did side effects from Agent Orange cause the aneurysm? He enjoyed life and made decisions with confidence. I missed the lessons on making good economic decisions that he and his wife, with a moderate income, always shared. I missed our common sense conversations about life in general and overcoming disappointments. I also missed his firm tone. I was the youngest sibling, and he was proud of me being the first family member to graduate from college—Clemson University with a master's degree. I sometimes thought that he intentionally gave my sister and me a hard time, but oftentimes, we would hear from other people how proud he was of us. He had maintained the legacy that our family shared by loving, caring, and supporting one another. We had lost another patriarch. Soon, funeral arrangements were being made; family members from out of town were contacted and friends offered their condolences.

In the meanwhile, my husband had accepted a new pastorate and was already living in Delaware. Our son was planning to further his education at Delaware State University with many details not yet finalized. We were 564 miles,

8 hours and 43 minutes, away from my husband. While waiting for the scheduling of Gary's funeral service, almost daily I would make call after call to DSU trying to get campus housing arranged for our son. There was a laundry list of small details not finalized before he could move on campus (i.e., high school and college transcripts and medical records, confirmation of a food plan and residential housing). Oftentimes, the telephone lines would be busy, or the person in charge of housing would not be available.

Traditionally, in the South during times of bereavement visitors would stop by, bringing food, and offering other services to the family of the deceased. One Sunday, while sitting in her family room, my sister-in-law asked me to come into the kitchen to meet several of her high school classmates. When I entered the room, she introduced me to one of her male classmates who was living in Delaware. The gentleman was also employed at DSU in campus housing. He and I began to talk and I shared with him that I had a son who would be attending the university in the fall and needed to live on campus. Within minutes, things began to fall into place. He was exceptionally helpful. Along with walking me through the procedure for completing paper work, the gentleman assured me that he would personally deliver our son's documents for processing. I felt like an albatross had flown off my shoulders. Not only was my grief lifted, but also a solution to a major concern had arrived from 564 miles, 8 hours and 43 minutes away, right into my sister-in-law's kitchen. The intervention I experienced in my sister-in-law's kitchen relieved my stress. It afforded me an opportunity to turn from what had taken days and hours to achieve into making important decisions in minutes. My grief transitioned to *gain*. Although death is still a mystery, my faith provided me light. I understood that my brother's death served as a bridge to allow my family and me to accomplish some much-desired goals. I began to realize that through death, he was released from pain and suffering. I reflect on the scripture Romans 8:28, which says, "And we know that all things work together for good to them that love God, to them who are the called according to his purpose" (KJV). Ten years has passed, but others who have had similar experiences, from time to time, will ask for my advice. Based on my experience and religious belief, I always encourage them to first pray about their situation and surround themselves with positive people. Then, I recommend that they never lose sight of their goal. Next, I motivate them to ask God to increase their faith. Lastly, I employ them to wait with patience, even in the darkest hour, for an answer.

Today, along with his three adult sons, there are two generations in our family that live with the name Gary. I resolved that while the death of my brother had appeared to be a nightmare, it was through his death that God sent an angel to assist with our relocation plans. Even now, when I think back on that moment, I get goose bumps. Through this experience, my faith has been increased, and I find myself working harder to always chase after the strength to use patience and wisdom when faced with challenges; I seek to hear from God. I am beginning to learn to live life to the fullest because I realize that even in the bleakest hour, decisions can be made in five minutes, or less, that can take my life into directions with promise.

Chapter 15

The beautiful life

by Raining Deer

At birth I was called Jeanette, the tenth of my mother's eleven children and the third of my father's four daughters. Mother worked as a housekeeper for thirty years in our small southern New Jersey town, and then got a job at the hospital where I was born right after she had me. I was the first of her children to be born in an actual medical facility up north rather than at home with a midwife in the Georgia countryside.

Mother always said the nurses delivered me because the doctor was late. Perhaps her child-birthing experience was the reason she thought highly of nurses and spoke as if she would be pleased if nursing became my career choice once I finished high school.

I was a very literate child; the Bible was my first book of study, as my godmother/Aunt Doll—my mother's sister—always insisted we read it together daily. My ability to read well took hold in primary school. A delightfully spirited, happy-go-lucky person who helped mother raise me, Aunt Doll would always say, "You're smart; you can be anything you want to be."

Another very important woman in my early life was my second grade teacher, Miss Campbell. She was from Mississippi and had a slight southern accent. She was the tallest, most beautiful lady I had ever seen, with chestnut brown skin, thick bouncy black hair like Marlo Thomas in *That Girl*, and a nice figure with long legs that had hair on them—you could see it through her stockings. Most of the boys at school thought she was beautiful too, and they developed crushes, giggling whenever she was around. I just liked her and she liked me because I was smart.

Miss Campbell gave me high school level books to take home so I could practice reading and vocabulary. It was a lot of fun, especially when it allowed me to become the teacher's pet. I soon found that Miss Campbell could teach me a lot more than my godmother could, due to her limited education. But with the combination of Aunt Doll's encouragement and Miss Campbell's instruction, writing became second nature for me.

However, third grade brought about changes. School desegregation had just gone into effect, which meant I had to be bussed across town. Why? Because the school nearest to my house was closed because the children from the other side of town weren't coming to my integrated neighborhood for school—their parents just wouldn't have it.

My third grade teacher, Miss Mason, was nice but she probably had a lot on her plate and didn't have any extra time to give to a common big-eyed, little girl with big words dancing through her brain. Soon the poetry I created for Miss Campbell was a lost memory. I blended in with the rest of the kids, learning cursive writing and playing on the swing at recess, always the highlight of my day.

Fourth grade and yet another school would luckily reconnect me with Miss Campbell. Yes—God himself intervened! The first thing she asked when she saw me was, "Are you still writing?" "What do you mean," I asked, not having the foggiest idea of what she was talking about. A child's attention span is so short.

Miss Campbell was horrified. "You used to write beautiful poems for me, and you read everything!" She couldn't believe her star pupil had not only stopped developing the gift she had worked so hard to hone, but her little apprentice didn't even remember ever writing anything special for her.

Perhaps it had to do with other things going on in my young life. Prior to my fifth birthday, I started having vivid revelations of events that had not yet happened, but when they did, I knew immediately that I had seen these occurrences—in my dreams. What was so disturbing was that they were about situations involving people I knew. Because I was so young, I was afraid to tell anyone. I'd overhear adults talking about these events once they happened, fearing that somehow I may have been the cause.

The visions probably impacted how I would later see events; but once I accepted that I had this gift and that it was normal for me, I would still get indications of future occurrences. However, instead of seeing the actual persons, I would see someone who had similar qualities—either physical or personal characteristics of those involved.

Miss Campbell and school were probably welcome distractions from my strange dreams. With school and my teacher I didn't have to think about feelings of guilt over the stuff that was happening to people while I slept. Even though I really had no control over the events, my young mind didn't understand, and I dared not tell her. But I did begin the writing process again, to Miss Campbell's delight and a great source of my present gratitude.

At age sixteen, the gift changed. Rather than dream about impending doom, I would think hard about someone I wanted to see, and they'd show up. I felt a great sense of mental power and control. This just became the norm for me and I went on with my life.

As high school graduation neared, my desire to please Mom heightened. She worked so hard for her children—cleaning hospital rooms, mopping floors, and never complaining about anything. Fulfilling her aspiration to have a nurse for a daughter weighed heavily on me. It was the least I could do.

A few months before graduation, I responded to a recruitment letter from a paramedic school. Being in the top 25 percent of my class meant I'd have no shortage of invitations to colleges. Biscayne Paramedical Institute was appealing because it was on the east coast but almost as far away from New Jersey as I could get without going north into colder weather. The program included specialized training for medical assistants and laboratory technicians. "Close enough," I thought. And with Mother's blessing, my mind was made up. Miami, here I come!

In 1977 when I left New Jersey for Miami—the Magic City—I began to live what I call "the beautiful life."

While paramedic studies was my initial reason for selecting Miami, I was on my own and making decisions for myself. I soon chose to try my hand at fashion and entertainment, modeling, and performance arts on the side. I ended up being a principle performer with a company that produced musical Broadway-type shows combining theater, dance, and fashion. Becoming a standout in a mediocre dance group was both fun and flattering, but I reached a crossroads when fans started to encourage me to go to New York where they thought I could really shine. Little did they know that singing and dancing were never serious considerations for me. I was just enjoying the freedom of being a young woman on her own for the first time in her life, calling the shots, yet still not sure of what I wanted to do with myself.

Nevertheless, everything was enjoyable for a few years. I lip-synced to Diana Ross tunes dressed in fabulous glittering dresses, danced to music from *Cabaret* and *West Side Story*, appeared in elegant modeling sequences that lowered me onto the stage in a swirling chandelier, and was the finale star in a *Bubbling Brown Sugar* number where I actually sang "It Don't Mean a Thing (If It Ain't Got That Swing)."

All was good until I got a rude indication that being a star performer was not to be my life path. It came in the form of heart attack symptoms that lingered a couple of weeks—long enough for me to take the hint that the universe had something else in store for me. I then turned back to what may be considered a talent; at least it was something that came natural to me. It was the ability that Miss Campbell saw in that little ingénue, inquisitive thinker—writing.

Rivers of My Mind was my first self-published work, a collection of poetry and prose that reflected my political observations, religious study, and that I was keenly aware of my personal interaction with spirit guides and their influence in my writing styles. I designed, printed, and marketed *Rivers*, doing readings and autograph sessions at bookstores and schools. I even got a positive response from a letter of inquiry sent to Essence magazine indicating they were interested in publishing one of my poems. It didn't happen—but at least they called! For an unknown, first-time, self-published author who had just decided that she wanted to be a writer that is, as Donald Trump would say, "HUUUUGE!" At least it was for my ego and self-confidence.

South Florida was very much an open landscape, full of opportunity. So when I got the chance to write for some local newspapers, I went for it and, as a result, the trajectory of my life would drastically change. Miami was my home, and one of its favorite adopted sons at the time was about to become my subject, then a client, a spiritual connection, and finally a really good friend.

It was the summer of 1985, and I had just returned from my first trip to Paris, France, which had proven to be everything I imagined, and more—big, beautiful, enchanting, romantic, and delightful—a writer's dream. I absolutely loved everything about Paris, and it would become a favorite destination.

I had been reporting for two local newspapers, one in Miami and one in Fort Lauderdale. I'd write community news articles, movie reviews, and social commentary. I had also co-founded a writers' workshop—an eclectic group of Miami artists comprised of writers, poets, theatrical performers and producers, musicians, painters, and educators.

There would eventually be spin-offs of the group into other cultural arts organizations, but our most influential contribution to South Florida was the Annual Pan African

Bookfest and Cultural Arts Conference. The institution we founded to produce this event was the African American Caribbean Cultural Arts Commission, Inc., and I became its executive director. We invited literary giants in the African diaspora to come and share their works with the Miami cultural community, and simultaneously gave a platform to showcase the works of visual and performing artists. Local musicians and other artists had the opportunity to hear and witness each other's mastery, sometimes resulting in collaboration, and always increasing appreciation and reverence for the genius of people of color—be they African American, Caribbean, Native American, Hawaiian, continental African, or Hispanic. We were one.

In August 1985, following my return from Paris, the editor of one of the papers asked me to cover a story. Apparently a police organization was having an annual ball, and they planned to present an award to Philip Michael Thomas, one of the stars of NBC's new hit show *Miami Vice.* I remembered him starring in the movie *Sparkle,* opposite Irene Cara in 1976, and since then I liked him as an actor.

At the time *Miami Vice* transformed the image of the television cop show due to its bold colors and dramatic beginning. Its pilot show focused on Thomas's character, Ricardo Tubbs, embarking on a mission to avenge the death of his older brother who had been gunned down by a drug lord named Calderon. The Calderon character would reappear in several episodes until Tubbs and Crockett (played by Don Johnson) teamed up and finally got their man.

In 1984 there hadn't been a black actor who was a bona fide sex symbol with a starring role in a television drama. Prior to then, Bill Cosby starred in *I Spy* (1965–1968),

Clarence Williams III starred in *The Mod Squad* (1968–1973), and Cuban-American Georg Stanford Brown co-starred in *The Rookies* (1972–1976). Denzel Washington had just started to gain notoriety for his portrayal of Dr. Chandler with the ensemble cast of *St. Elsewhere*, which made George Clooney a star. Whether Cosby, Williams, and Stanford Brown were actually considered male sex symbols at that time is debatable, but the inability to ethnically pigeonhole Thomas probably gave him broader appeal. Coupled with the chemistry between him and costar Johnson made for the show's meteoric success.

Still, I did not want to cover the policemen's ball. "He's not going to show up. It's MTV on steroids. He's not coming!" I protested.

That plus the facts that I'd have to get dressed up and go alone to a ball were enough excuses for not covering this story. The editor wasn't hearing any of it. He begged me to go. So, I got all gussied up and went to the ball at the DuPont Plaza Hotel, a landmark that had the distinction of being the first big modern hotel in the soon-to-be hub of the Caribbean—downtown Miami. It also happened to be where I had attended classes at Biscayne Paramedical Institute. I was coming full circle.

While beginning to show its age, the DuPont was still a posh venue for hosting celebrity events. You could sense its former grandeur, perched at the mouth of the Miami River where it poured into Biscayne Bay. I also covered a program there featuring heavyweight boxing champ Muhammad Ali and then Ambassador Andrew Young.

Their stories were only minor snippets in the catalog of newsmakers and celebrities that began to fill my journalistic portfolio. I was soon writing feature articles on the first black city manager of the city of Miami and corporate CEOs, as well as controversial figures like Minister Louis Farrakhan, and music icons Michael Jackson, Prince, George Michael, and The Bee Gees, with some of the stories garnering front page headlines. Several years later I would be enlisted to help a group of entrepreneurs create a magazine format, and I became its editor in chief.

Back at the DuPont Hotel, on the scheduled night I entered the ballroom and surveyed what looked like an expansively elegant banquet hall. I found a seat in the center of the room not far from the dance floor. The newly appointed chief of police was a few tables across the room, so I made my way over to get a quick comment about his new job and the attention that a TV crime drama was bringing to his city.

In those days, network television was still king. Cable had not yet become the ratings competitor that it is today with media titans HBO, Showtime, and the like pulling viewers from ABC, CBS, and NBC. As a result, popular shows on the big three networks made mega stars of actors who had the fortune of landing leading roles. It was Lifestyles of the Rich and Famous for real.

After returning to my table, I settled down for what I thought would be an uneventful night. People filtered in lazily and anticipation was modest. This was apparently an annual gala, and the organization members were somewhat enthusiastic, but the evening seemed to get off to a slow start.

Just as the program got underway, a small group of people arrived at the table directly in front of me. A tall attractive woman (reminiscent of Miss Campbell) dressed in black was accompanied by a fairly big man, who was a tall handsome guy with brown curly hair, wearing a white evening jacket. They moved with precision, giving cover to another white tuxedo-clad man who was not as big or as tall as the other two. As they seated themselves, I realized the group was an entourage, and Philip Michael Thomas was at its center.

"Well!" I thought, "He actually showed up. Bernie Dyer (my editor) will be pleased."

At that point, people were still milling around, not noticing that the guest of honor had arrived. How quickly things change. I decided to take the civil approach, thinking that rather than just be the intrusive reporter and start tossing questions at the man, I'll ask politely. I lifted my petite, slight frame from my seat, walked over to the guest table, and knelt down beside him.

"Mr. Thomas, I'm with the *Miami Weekly* newspaper. I don't want to disturb you, but would you mind giving me a few minutes of your time after the program?

"Sure," he said. He was quite agreeable.

"I'm sitting at the table just behind you, so I'll see you when you're all finished," I advised.

He looked over to my empty seat, making sure he knew where I'd be, and said,

"Okay, I look forward to speaking with you."

That was simple enough, I thought as I pranced back to my seat feeling confident that my "polite" strategy had worked.

Soon the program was in full swing. Early on, the emcee made the mistake of announcing that Philip Michael Thomas was there. A buzz turned into a hmmmm, and heads began to turn, spying the room to see where he was seated. Whenever searching eyes landed on me, just shy of the target, I sensed the disappointment, which emoted "You're not him—get out of my sightline!" I was amused.

Once discovered, Thomas's table became a magnet and a surge of mostly women started to make their way over to him.

Seeing that things might get out of hand, the emcee seemed to move up the award presentation to an earlier time in the program lineup. He brought Thomas to the stage to thundering applause, and what I sensed as somewhat of a seismic clap.

I knew there were many of them in the ballroom, but after he ascended to the stage, I'm pretty sure women dropped out of helicopters, jumped out of speed boats, fell off of buses, and traversed mountainsides (by the way—there are no mountains anywhere in the state of Florida); I'm just saying they appeared out of nowhere. The program had to be temporarily preempted, and I thought I'd never get my interview.

The small security detail ushered Thomas back to his table in an attempt to allow the program to go forward. The women had other ideas.

The next thing I see is Thomas and his team rising from the table, shifting their attention towards the outer lobby. As they passed by my table he looked my way, and I quickly asked, "Are you leaving?"

He responded, "No, but can you come out here?"

"Sure," I replied.

He was led out to a large, long lobby area that ran the length of the ballroom. The women followed, clamoring for an autograph, a feel of his hands, his clothing, and his hair. They were almost hysterical. I watched nonchalantly as I leaned against the back of a conveniently positioned couch.

I don't know who was left in the ballroom, but all the action was taking place in the lobby, and it seemed to go on and on.

Suddenly, I felt a hand clasp mine, pulling me to the center of the mayhem. It was Mr. Thomas. I don't know how he found my hand through the hoard of dancing estrogen, but I was ever the pro, as spontaneous as I needed to be.

"Are we leaving?" I asked.

"Yes," he responded.

As we hurried through the open glass doors, a gold-colored Mercedes awaited. We practically dove into the backseat, the doors quickly closing behind us, quieting the cackle of the crowd.

I'm sure the ball organizers were glad that we were gone so they could get on with the show.

Back in the car, we made our way down Brickell Avenue heading to the Mutiny Hotel, a popular spot back in the day situated in an artsy, wealthy area of Miami known as Coconut Grove, which had been settled by Bahamian settlers in the city's early days. Brickell turned into the beautiful palm lined Bayshore Drive with modest homes of wealthy Miamians on one side, Biscayne Bay on the other. It would later have its share of scandals and homicides—the stuff you see on CBS's *48 Hours* or NBC's *Dateline*.

I took out my notepad and began my interview.

"How did you get started in the entertainment industry?" was my first question.

"I entered a talent show singing "Rockin' Robin," was Thomas's response, followed by him actually singing the song. Of course I joined in. Who could resist singing "Rockin' Robin" with a TV star!

When we arrived at The Mutiny, the rest of the security team got out and left us to finish the interview. Mr. Thomas was extremely open and personable, telling me about his whole journey from a San Francisco production of *Hair* to Broadway, to guest appearances on popular sitcoms and TV dramas such as *Starsky & Hutch, Trapper John M.D., Good Times*, and more. There was an immediate connection that was effortless and I would soon conclude, predestined.

"Would you come with me up to my suite? I'd like to introduce you to my mother," he asked.

I almost lost my breath, thinking, "Is this really happening?" And then, "Is he okay?" But as quickly as I processed the situation—that a police officer was downstairs waiting to take me back to my car, and after all *it was his mother*, so I wouldn't be totally alone with him; I concluded it was okay to push out, "Of course, I'd love to meet your mother."

As we began our walk down a long corridor to the hotel elevator, our hands were wrapped together tightly. It was surreal as I felt a surge of electricity running from his hand into mine. Halfway down the hall, Mr. Thomas turned to me and said, "Do you feel that?" I couldn't believe he said exactly what I was thinking, as I exclaimed, "Yes, you feel it too?" The night was getting crazier by the moment.

We continued to the elevator, up to his apartment where I met Mrs. Thomas, his mother who was as lovely a lady as you would ever want to meet, and incidentally also a writer.

So I was shuttled off in the back of a gold Mercedes in beautiful tropical Miami singing "Rockin' Robin" with one of America's hottest television stars of the day. The night would end with me in his temporary residence overlooking the deep, blue waters of Biscayne Bay, meeting his mother, him sharing with me a cassette tape of some of his original music, and—I almost forgot, his phone number—and of course I shared mine. It was the beginning of a beautiful and continuing relationship.

There were more beautiful and productive relationships to come. I would soon meet a Native American shaman who I would marry on a Florida Seminole Reservation. Yes, that somewhat explains my pen name Raining Deer. Together we would conceive a son who continues to be a medicine carrier—the embodiment of a love fulfilled and a blessing to me. But that path is yet another chapter in my storied life.

Looking back over thirty years, my decision to go to Miami was the right decision. It was vibrant, alive, exciting, nourishing, soothing, and balanced. It was paradise with bright sunshine, natural beauty, and mangos and avocados hitting my slanted rooftop like missiles; lemon, orange, and grapefruit trees in my back yard; and spiritual food truly feeding my soul, as did my Miami family, all predestined to cross my path and I theirs.

Ultimately my decision to follow what came passionately, organically, and with ease—writing—made an enormous difference in the future that became my colorful and exciting journey, one which, as Philip Michael Thomas always says, is still *to be continued.*

Chapter 16

Designing my destiny

by Dell Scott

I had no idea, that in a matter of five minutes, one's life can change forever. Sitting in my chair, I mentally drifted back in time, remembering dreams and aspirations that I desired for my life. I always wanted to live a life without regrets. Naturally, the expected life I was to lead took its course. I matured, married, and started a family. I also had a good job as an accountant in a family business. I just could not figure out why everything I had in life was not enough for me. I asked myself, "Why am I not fulfilled?" "Is it selfish of me to feel this way?" As days passed, those questions began to plague me. I had reached nearly fifteen years on the job and was pining at the fact that there was more to my life than what I was living—there was actually more to who I was. I knew I was more than just a wife, mother, sister, daughter, and an employee. Have you ever felt that there was so much more you had to offer to the world? I did.

Added to the midst of life's trials, were the physical scars of being born with eczema. The physical scars that ultimately became mental scars. Those scars played a big part of the mindset that stopped me from doing what I was truly passionate about. That passion was working in the fashion world. I believed in my heart that I had something to offer, but my scars told me differently. Every time I looked at my skin, I felt lack of self-love, low self-esteem, and lack of confidence. All of those issues became my reflection when I looked in the mirror. I ultimately felt that I did not fit society's standard for what beauty exemplified. I always compared myself to other girls that I thought were prettier or more stylish. No one would ever know that for many years I desired to completely change how I looked, because I could not embrace how God created me.

A desire I always held on to was the passion for fashion at an early age. There was nothing like the turn of a page from a fashion magazine or the feeling that playing dress-up gave me . . . yes, nothing could compare to that. I could no longer deny what I felt inside, and in 2008, the legacy of Divacoutoure began. I wanted to create a "tour de fashion" for all women to experience. I wanted to provide showstopper shoes, upscale apparel, and exquisite jewelry that appealed to the unique individuality of every woman. The purpose of Divacoutoure transcended into a mission to "empower women to unleash their inner diva." What I thought was only to be fashion retail evolved into a multifaceted fashion company, offering fashion services as well. I started to move into my true calling as a stylist and then ultimately a designer. As a stylist, I have found joy in seeing women further enhance the beauty they already possess. As a designer, I have been able to create unique designs that capture the very essence of a woman. It was laid on my heart to enlarge my fashion platform by designing The DS Collection. The DS Collection is custom femme fashion for the woman who knows the brilliance she possesses. The collection embodies designs for women that are unique and desire to make a statement when they walk into a room. When women wear my designs, I want them to feel just as brilliant on the inside as they do on the outside. Because we are in a society that portrays such false pretenses, it was my desire to get women back to displaying the true essence of women. As a designer, I feel that essence is grace, elegance, and class. After being blessed to participate in popular fashion week events, I look forward to taking my collection to higher heights.

I have come to realize that amazing things happen when you make the decision to do what you are purposed to do. Through my fashion platform, God not only enabled me to help women with the same issues that I once carried, but he enabled me to embrace myself along the way. I have crossed paths with women that, just like me, felt they were not beautiful. I have been blessed with the ability to help them embrace their outer being.

Little did I know, this was only the tip of the iceberg of what God had called me to do in my life. My platform began to open doors for me as a writer and a speaker. With two new platforms to stand on, I began to write articles and speak on the importance of image. I began to tackle image not only with fashion attire but also with the power of a pen. God began to show me that I must focus on the inner being of a woman as much as her outer being. I began to delve into the mental mindset of image, as well as the visual, to help women truly accept themselves. Initially, this was a painful experience, because I was forced to relive moments from my childhood. I remembered the pain of losing my hair, being teased about my physical scars, and feeling like an "ugly duckling." It is something about putting your experiences into words that can make them come to life all over again. I grew to become just as passionate about writing as I did about styling/designing. I continued to press forward, encouraged by the women who were touched by my stories. Did they have any idea that their feedback was encouraging me at the same time my story was encouraging them? I wondered. My purpose had now expanded from enhancing women's outer beauty into showing women how to believe in themselves and realize they were made in excellence.

Here I was again, back in the chair, reliving the path I had taken in life up to that point. I was in awe over the moments I had experienced and the life-changing decisions I had made. It was one of those very moments that led up to September of 2013. That was when God laid it on my heart to write *The Undiscovered Jewel, Realizing the Brilliance That Lies Within*. He told me I needed to write the book for *all* women—women of all cultures, backgrounds, and socio-economic statuses. He stressed that we are living in a society that is riddled by the allure of Hollywood lights and reality TV. These environments were causing women to have an identity crisis in the natural realm.

God gave me the revelation that we, as women, are all comparable to diamonds. We possess the same beauty, brilliance, and preciousness. Women have their own unique cut, rare clarity, radiant color, and specific carat weight in this walk called life. The cutting process of a diamond is a crucial aspect to its final beauty. Likewise the "cutting process" we go through in our lives (our life experiences) are all unique according to what we are purposed to do in this world. There are no two women alike; we have our own distinct features and our own radiant color, just as they are no two diamonds created the same. Just because a blemish or an inclusion might affect a diamond's clarity, it does not mean the gem does not have value. God wants us to realize that those outside scars or sensitive areas that we have do not diminish the brilliance that he has placed inside us. We have our own weight to carry in this life, just like a diamond naturally has its own specific carat weight. God wants us to stop searching for what we think is brilliance and realize that we already possess it.

In a moment of despair, I almost did not complete *The Undiscovered Jewel.* I became distraught because I felt I could not offer something impactful. Moments of feeling like I was not qualified or I did not have anything to say of value tried to fill my mind. In an era where we have many authors, writers, coaches, and speakers, I had to know without a shadow of a doubt that what I was writing was going to help my fellow women. I did not want to write meaningless words on paper just to claim an author status. I wanted every woman that read my book to walk away truly embracing who she was. There were moments where I was frustrated and angry. I wanted to give up but I heard the words "keep writing" in my spirit. I pushed past how I felt and was able to complete the book. If you could only imagine the tears that were shed as I held the first copy in my hands. I could not have possibly imagined the immense positive feedback and encouragement from the release of the book. The heart-filled words spoken by readers were enough to confirm in my spirit that I did what I was purposed to do, and did it well.

I have come to realize that it is not the moments in our

lives that define us, but ultimately the decisions we make during those moments. Do we give up or do we press forward? In my moments, I choose to press forward! I choose to be *everything* God has called me to be and do *everything* God has placed me in this universe to do!

part three

BARS: action

Chapter 17

Action

by Nancy Fox

"If you don't love what you do, you won't do it with much conviction or passion." Mia Hamm

What is your power or force? Action is the verb in your life—the influence you have by doing something, or a movement in your life that spreads into the world.

Maroon 5 (pop music group) decided to take their music into the weddings of a handful of couples on December 6, 2014. Their video gained much attention from the implementation, but the action taken created so much more for the couples that received the gift. Surprising a few people, making memorable moments, or supporting someone through a difficult time is action that influences the world.

Maroon 5 shared their talents in a very special way. What are your talents? What do you believe about your talents? Are they worthy of giving to others? Many women may doubt their worthiness, but they know in their deep core that they have valuable actions to take in order to share their talents. Are you taking action that shares your talents in a special way?

Your beliefs, your desired benefits, and now the action you must take go together to get what you want. Be clear on what it is that you want. Is it physical, emotional, or spiritual? The benefit you get from taking action may be one or more of these types of benefits. If the action gets you a physical benefit, there will most likely be an emotional response connected to it. Spiritual benefits require a deeper need and may be linked with an emotional need, although it is not unthinkable that receiving a physical benefit may lead to a spiritual benefit. This spiritual benefit may be experienced in a healing or a situation resolved that is totally out of your control. The only way to describe the event is through a spiritual experience.

Think of the benefit that you want. Describe it in specific detail. Think of one step you can take to get what you want. For someone it may be simply to get up out of bed today and get dressed to help overcome an illness or a moment of loss in her life. For others the benefit could be to see a family member, friend, or someone they haven't seen in a long time. This benefit will only take place if the motivation/movement/action to reach that person is initiated. For still others, the benefit may be to reach a financial goal that gives them the ability to serve others in a way not imagined prior to taking action in a sponsorship, a business venture, or a savings plan to achieve the benefit. I don't know what benefit you are striving to gain. You do. Make that first step and decide on the next step. Like babies, who intuitively know that one day they will be just like the people standing and moving around them, they take the necessary action to make the standing, walking, and running part of their action plans.

When I was sick with Lyme disease I literally could not get off the couch for a period of time. Many others have suffered far more than I have from Lyme disease, so this analogy is simply my experience. Getting from the couch to the bathroom was exhausting and nearly impossible. The moment I realized my physical inability to put one foot in front of the other to get to the benefit I desired was a day I will not forget. My mind wanted to move in that direction but my body would not coordinate to achieve that benefit. In my mind I knew I had the skills to move/take action to get to where I had decided to go but my body didn't fulfill that action. I was stuck. I had to look for support from an expert, someone who could walk with me from one place to another, with the ability to get to my desired place/benefit.

If you do not have the skills you need to get the benefit you want, find the experts to get those skills. Take action. Maybe you have the skills but you don't have the ability to get to the benefit. Again take action. Find someone or something that will assist you to get to the benefit you desire. Do not stop taking action until you have fulfilled the desire of your heart and get what you want. If you look around you and admire someone because of that person's successes, then you must ask that person about his or her journey to success. Remember that person's belief system, benefit list, and actions may not match with yours. You will find the BARS in their journey if you listen carefully. You may also find that some people may not be able to describe their BARS from their journey. Some people have used their success strategy for so long that it is ingrained in the body, mind, and spirit. It may take them time to think about it. The key to listen for is the action they took in order to get the benefits they have received.

Action is the one thing every entrepreneur focuses on. Sure, selling lots of products or services makes the entrepreneur feel great about one's influence and message that is being heard. However, if the consumer doesn't use the information or product to fulfill a need, the influence stops and the purpose is not maximized. Have you ever received a product or service and didn't follow the prescribed action? Sure, we all have done that at least once along our journey in life. Or we followed the prescribed action for a time period, got the results we were looking for, and stopped taking action. What actions are you taking that are not being maximized? Are the actions you are taking making a positive difference in your life and/or in the lives of others? Are the connections you are making touching lives and, in turn, touching someone else's life in a positive manner?

Ladies, have you noticed we are taking the world by storm? The numerous women who are designing their lives are right before your eyes. Those who have shared the following stories have taken action despite difficult circumstances and have made a decision to take a step towards their desires with passion and persistence.

- As you look to the notable women in your life, how do you think they got where they are at this point of their lives? Ask one of the women to describe her path to her destiny. Does she answer the question in the way you perceived, or does she have a different response?

- Women are emerging as a driving force in business, nonprofit organizations, healthcare, entertainment, and within their families and communities. People like Oprah Winfrey have taken the power of women to the children by partnering with other countries and businesses to provide schools and opportunities never imagined by the girls living in their particular culture. How can you affect the landscape of the community where you desire a greater good for women and children?

Chapter 18

The "Be Positive" formula

by Elayna Fernandez

Do you wish you could enjoy more passion in your life and know that every time adversity, pain, and loss happens you could adopt a positive outlook to propel you forward with greater power than you ever thought you had?

As a woman who has made many decisions to consciously design the life I want, I have learned to fill my life with joy, balance, and success on my own terms, and to teach other moms to do the same.

It all starts with awareness, noticing your thoughts, questioning your thoughts, and reframing your thoughts. I developed three principles that bring more awareness to guide my thinking and therefore guide my life towards empowering choices that create happiness each day.

I was seven years old when I first used this formula. Growing up as one of the poorest kids in town in the Dominican Republic, my toys were often items others considered trash. One particular day, I found a soggy, smelly magazine among the waste. It immediately caught my eye, and as I glanced through the pages, I saw the happy faces of kids that had everything I needed and everything I ever wanted. I decided I was going to pursue the life of the kids in the *Highlights* magazine, and that the first step to do that was to learn English so I could decipher how.

Let's study these principles.

Find a treasure in the dump. Your history and your circumstances do not define you. Maybe up until now . . . and right now, all you see is debris all around, but if you believe you are worth a treasure and stay around long enough to seek it, you will indeed find it.

Maybe you're thinking: *Oh, that's easy for you to say! You have no idea where I've been, what I've done, or what I've been through!* And you're right, I don't. But I know that in this human experience we all share, we all have what I call defining moments, moments in which you have the divine opportunity to define yourself and not let the moment define you.

As Alice in Wonderland said, "Who in the world am I? Ah, that's the great puzzle."

I have been in the dump, literally and figuratively, and I believed that was my destiny, and even worse, my identity. Do not let your dump fool you. Your dump is a training ground for the greatness that awaits your shero journey. Think of the refiner's fire or the pressure on the coal that makes it a diamond. You are a goddess in training. Before you make any decision, remind yourself who you are, what you are worth, and the grand destination that awaits you.

A great tool to see beyond your own personal dump is to get in a state of gratitude by acknowledging what you have.

I borrowed a Theodore Roosevelt quote and adopted it as my mantra: "Do what you can, with what you have, where you are."

No matter what you are, there is something you have, something you can do, because you have infinite unused power within you. Start recognizing that you are worth it, that you are enough, and that you have the power to choose to live by design and not by default. When you look at your mistakes, your regrets, your unwanted past and present circumstances, and say to yourself: *I am more than that,* you actually tune in to a field of infinite ideas and have the ability to listen to the still, small voice that will guide you to the life you've always wanted. I like the words of Napoleon Hill: "Every adversity, every failure, every heartache carries with it the seed of an equal or greater benefit."

Access a vision of what could be possible. It says in the Bible that all it takes is a tiny seed of faith to move mountains. Sometimes faith comes to us in the manner of curiosity.

It's been said that the quality of our lives is often equal to the quality of the questions we consistently ask. I've found that a great tool to ignite faith is asking the question: "What if," because it activates your imagination beyond what you know, challenging your perception of truth and reality, and accessing greater possibilities.

We tend to make decisions by relying on what we see, what we hear, what we smell, what we can touch, and what we can taste. We make great use of our five senses, yet we often underutilize our six mental faculties: reason, memory, perception, will, intuition, and imagination.

"What if?" is the gate to listening to your self and discovering that conventional wisdom, at times, just isn't wisdom at all.

Absence of evidence isn't evidence of absence. There are infallible, yet invisible, laws at work at all times, and these dictate your everyday results. As you work in alignment with these laws, you will start to see the imminent evidence in your life . . . not the other way around.

Just as a little bit of light can dispel the deepest darkness, as you let a tiny seed of possibility in, you will be enlightened with a vision, empowered with guidance, and equipped with exactly what you need to see it come true.

Decide *how* you will be. Have you gotten a glimpse of the plans God has for you? You've read that he has plans for you to prosper, yet you wonder how. And perhaps you've heard that if you know the why and the what, the "how" will take care of itself, but I actually believe that the "how" is the foundation to taking action toward your dream.

This is the key question: Are you asking "How on Earth?" or are you asking "How can I?" And furthermore, are you dismissing your answer?

As a decisive woman, I often wanted to know how the story would end, how every piece fit into the puzzle, and the "how" to each step before getting started.

Dr. Martin Luther King, Jr., a man who is famous for having one of the noblest dreams we know, said, "Take the first step in faith. You don't have to see the whole staircase, just take the first step."

Any journey, no matter how long it may seem, starts with one single step. And sometimes the step we must take is actually the least obvious because it doesn't fit into what we know or know about.

Let me tell you another time when I used this formula in my life. I woke up at 3:00 a.m. and found myself left as a single mom of two toddlers, after a little over three years of marriage. I had left my homeland, my corporate career, my loving family, my supportive friends, and everything I knew, and now I was alone and ashamed, without a penny to my name, stuck in a one-room efficiency without a kitchen, in a small town of South Florida. I didn't have a job or a car; I didn't even know how to drive! Curled up in the fetal position, feeling sorry for myself, I started questioning everything, including my worth. I felt I had nothing, and my life was surely over.

History repeats itself, and at times, more than we'd like it to. Here I was, two decades later, now in a deep personal dump, and I was inadvertently inspired to use the same formula that assisted me in creating success in my childhood years and beyond.

These three principles completely transformed my experience: I went from victim to victor in a matter of minutes. It was miraculous . . . and almost magical!

I looked beyond the dump and was able to see my little angel girls peacefully asleep, and I felt a wave of gratitude overcome me. It didn't seem I had much, yet I had the best part. I once again found a treasure in the dump!

"I will lift up mine eyes unto the hills, from whence cometh my help. My help cometh from the Lord" (Psalm 121:1–2, KJV).

Embodying one of my most meaningful identities (mom), I let my mental faculties take over and asked myself: "What if?"

What if my daughters didn't have to ever go through what I was going through?

What if my daughters could have the Highlights kids' childhood?

What if I could turn it all around and offer them a life of joy?

What if they could grow to have balance and success?

What if I could push an imaginary reset button and start anew, taking 100 percent responsibility for all my choices?

I started to visualize their entrepreneurial journeys, their joyful play, even their weddings! I could see it, I could hear it, and I could feel it. I started to believe it was possible for them . . . for us!

I didn't let the "how" show up on its own, I needed to know what I could do to make this happen or at least to make it welcome. I asked myself how, not as in: *How could I possibly do this without money, without my friends and family, without a clue on how to get started?* but as in: *How can I do this, where I am, with what I have?*

I'd like to tell you that I came up with a plan, but that was not the case. Instead, something strange happened. I started seeing images in my head from a movie I had watched and loved. It is called *Life Is Beautiful*, a multiple Academy Award winner film by Roberto Benigni. Now, I wanted to stop thinking about this and focus on a real issue, and kind of an important one!

Then I yielded, surrendered, and listened to the still small voice. I started to notice what it was trying to tell me. Here's the IMDB description for this 1997 movie: "When an open-minded Jewish librarian and his son become victims of the Holocaust, he uses a perfect mixture of will, humor and imagination to protect his son from the dangers around their camp."

Was I not going through my very own personal Holocaust? Did I not moments ago just feel like my daughters were stuck there with me? I reasoned: This was the answer to my prayer!

Will, I have. Humor, I have. Imagination, I have. I have everything I need. I am everything I need to be to overcome this!

I didn't know what I could or would do, but I knew what I could and would be. This was the first moment in my life in which instead of a "to-do list," I wrote a "to-be list," and my life has never been the same.

I decided to *be* empowered, to *be* faithful, to *be* joyful, to *be* committed . . . "Be positive and you will be powerful."

And I made a conscious decision of the mom I would be—a positive mom. I started the divine insight that took me through each step of the staircase, even when I didn't acknowledge it. Although people say the "how" will just show up, in my experience I found that each step of the "how" was revealed to me as I sought higher guidance.

The journey has been long, and the lessons have been many, but as I've become aware of this code to a life empowered, I have not only become more of what I am meant to be, but I have also given my daughters permission to do the same. They shine their light brighter than I ever imagined—they are who I saw in my vision and much more.

Being positive is not thinking you will live your vision in the absence of challenges or in the absence of fear. It is the certainty that through faith, gratitude, and willingness to work with the invisible side of your divine self, you can get to your grand, glorious destiny.

"When God gives you a vision, he gives you the provision."

Chapter 19

Walk away to win

by Laura Steward

I love to ask questions. Lots of questions. Not only of others but of myself too. My goal is to ask questions that surface answers that make me a little bit uncomfortable at the thought of what I would need to do with the answer. I want to ask questions to get the answers I need and not just the answers I want. If they match, even better!

Sometimes that path of questioning opens several forks in the road that can be chosen. Even doing nothing with the answers is a fork that opens possibilities and outcomes. I chose a fork during my very first job after college, and it has proven to be one that set a course in my life that was not something I had dreamed. All because I was willing to walk away from a job when I was being wronged.

Walk away without fighting for yourself? That's not something I was ever taught. I had learned that you needed to fight for what was right. Ask the right questions and outcomes will lay out in your favor. In the story I am about to tell you that was not a possibility.

I was a couple years out of college in what was a wonderful job working with amazing people. We all respected each other and supported each other. Men. Women. Didn't matter. If you had the skills for the job, you were respected in the position. Learning new skills was expected. Then, a new manager came in and everything changed for me.

What was a department where my ideas and talents were respected became a job where I was treated as a secretary versus a technical writer. I became a gofer and proofreader versus a member of the technical team writing field manuals and testing products before they went out the door.

I had graduated with a degree in computer science and was studying for a masters in management; yet, my new boss criticized everything I did. He wanted me to rewrite every memo that he wanted to send—his spelling and grammar were atrocious. And he asked me to justify every manual I had written that was in the field with huge success saying, "This is all garbage."

Every fiber of my being told me just wait it out, he won't last long. I spoke to my old management, the guys on the team, and other women in the division. They wouldn't believe me. They had not seen the behavior. He was always courteous and praising to them.

Not knowing what else to do, I decided to set up an experiment. I arranged with a few of the engineers in the department who were going to be with me in a staff meeting to pay attention to what happens when I offer ideas or speak in the meeting. Then, if my ideas were discredited or ignored, they were to wait a few minutes and state my ideas as if they were their own.

Do you have an idea what happened? Every time one of the male engineers gave my idea, they were told it was great and let's implement it. After about two hours in the meeting,

I grew so angry I stormed out of the conference room, seriously slamming doors. Not one of my best moments.

I went back to my office and tried to figure out my next step. The meeting broke up, and the engineers I had drafted into my plan found me. They couldn't believe what had happened. We went to management above my manager to tell them about what had happened. This part you will never believe. Or maybe you will. Management tried to turn it around and make it entirely my fault.

At that moment, I realized nothing I could prove would make any difference. There were politics at play higher than my influence. I'm not a quitter. Especially when I feel there is an injustice. This time I knew, in every fiber of my being, that I HAD to leave the company. That afternoon I sent my resume over to a friend at a larger company to see if there were any positions. The next day I had an interview, a job offer with more responsibilities, and a 30 percent increase in pay.

Here is the even funnier part: the job was targeted for a woman, and they had been looking for almost a year to find one with the qualifications. Mine exceeded every other candidate, male or female, who had applied. They were getting ready to reclassify the job when my resume crossed their desks. Timing.

I started the job two weeks later and never looked back. The discriminatory manager I left was still there two years later and had been promoted twice. Politics.

When I was asking myself questions about the situation I was in, I could have settled on the option to not make waves, let it all shake out, and hide my frustration. Something a lot of women would do since we are taught to be peacemakers.

Or, I could have looked for a different position inside the company or at the parent company. Why didn't I take either of those forks?

It came down to this. I respected myself too much for the first option, and the second option would still have me working for a company where it was acceptable for what I felt were discriminatory practices. This was long before most of the federal laws had been fully implemented to prevent situations like this from happening. Even with the laws in place, sometimes you have to walk away and say, where am I stronger?

For me, the stronger position was to walk away from a no-win situation with grace and a little bit of swagger since the new position was significantly better.

At the second company, I created opportunities that eventually led to my founding a multistate technology company, which I sold in 2009. Not a path I had planned. Yet one that then created a move to Florida and another career as an award-winning author and international speaker.

Walking away and not fighting for myself that day showed me that not fighting for what I believed was the right thing; sometimes it is the stronger position. You need to understand the entire picture and not just your perception of the picture. Once I had proved what I knew to be true and took it to upper management, I saw the other part of the picture. Politics.

Without the political influence, I would never win. What I would be doing if I had kept fighting was to create an eventually untenable position where I would have a stalled career.

As a caregiver to my eighty-six-year-old mother, I am learning different aspects of this lesson. I could keep correcting her when she does something wrong or when her memory has her telling people mixed-up stories from our life. Or, I can just let it go if it is not life threatening. I can let people who need to know the accurate information when my mom is not nearby, allowing her to have peace of mind versus worry and anxiety over her "my brain is asleep" (as she puts it) moments.

Stepping back allowed me to see the real facts of that first job and to move forward to a better position that opened doors I had never expected. I'm still working on the stepping back with mom consistently, though!

What questions are you asking yourself today? Do you find yourself in a situation that makes you feel like you are beating your head against a wall, the same wall? Without making forward progress? If you are, change the questions you are asking. See if there are doors if you take a few steps backwards or sideways from the wall. Perhaps there is an opportunity you haven't seen because you wanted to win or just make things right in your world.

My journey began long before that day I decided to walk away from the fight. I decided that winning, in that case, meant having a better career than the one I could ever have had there. Self-satisfaction and respect was more important than what that one manager thought of me. I knew what I could do and who I was.

The right questions can change your life. They changed, and continue to change, my clients and mine. What are you asking yourself?

Chapter 20

Zip code of the heart

by Tonya Joy

Standing in our truth isn't always easy, but there's a high price to pay for living anywhere except the ever-present, unchanging zip code of the heart.

Relationships—especially romantic ones—offer an immediate and exacting compass to gauge our alignment with our inner truth. They provide both an unbiased mirror of our current consciousness, as well as the rich, fertile soil for our emotional and spiritual growth. If we are fully present and open to seeing the abundant opportunities of this reflective landscape of love, we can stay centered in our hearts, blossom into our fullness, and more readily navigate the hills and valleys with gratitude, grace, and ease.

For as with the rest of life, romantic partnerships have their share of highs and lows. They are inevitable and inescapable—just like the seasons. It is our *presence* and our *perception* of these ever-changing vistas that determine our experience. For even when gnawing pain and gut-wrenching heartbreak are forefront and change is on the horizon, we can step forward with unwavering courage, childlike curiosity, and heartfelt compassion for ourselves, our lover, and life itself—*if we dare to stand in our truth.*

In 2012 I faced a grueling decision—whether to leave my partner of seventeen years or stick it out and live what felt like a diminished existence. It was a difficult, soul-stirring time as I wrestled with the undeniable disconnect between my heart and my head. I made lists of pros and cons, went to psychotherapy, and meditated. I did breath work, energy work, self-inquiry, and various other forms of process work. I challenged my thinking, healed past wounds, asked for divine guidance, and endured many honest, tearful conversations with my beloved as we did our best to arrive at an answer that felt true, compassionate, and loving—*for both of us.* It was anything but easy.

We had shared over half of our adult lives together, and though the years were filled with many challenges, we enjoyed a deep, beautiful love; a creative, respectful partnership; and a stone-solid friendship that was the bedrock of our lives. The thought of leaving ripped my heart out, yet the thought of staying devoured my soul.

The internal dialogues and sometimes exasperating discussions continued, as we felt an indescribable pressure to commit fully to our relationship or separate our lives. The process—though enlightening and helpful—was excruciating. Yet together, we learned to be transparent and vulnerable as we spoke our deepest, often untold, truths and listened (best we could) with receptive, nonjudging hearts and minds. This was homeschooling for adults—and the toughest education I've ever encountered! In the end, our report cards shined with star-encrusted "As" for patience, presence, and perseverance.

Yet despite the growth and insight, there were times when I thought my entire being would dissolve from the unrelenting pain. Gasping for air between breathless tears, I was convinced I would be reduced to a single, watery molecule and namelessly float away among what I called The Unstoppable Salty Rain. My soul mate and I were afloat on the stormy seas of life armed only with invisible oars of love and a sincere commitment to that which was highest for us both.

Together we rowed. Together we journeyed. Together we mounted the seemingly endless waves of emotion that threatened to engulf us, yet simultaneously held the gift of our freedom. Truth was our life raft, and we trusted it would deliver us to the shore (or shores) of our future. So together we paddled . . . one wet stroke at a time.

The weeks passed and the sun rose again and again to illuminate unresolved issues that lay dormant, yet ripe for excavation. We struggled—yet we survived. We laughed and cried and sometimes raged. We lived in honesty and drank the painful truth of our fears, failures, and frailties. At times, we cuddled compassionately as one heaved in grief (generally me) and the other sat in the seat of the wise and caring witness. All along, we burned up our stored pasts and built inner muscles we never knew we had. Then one day, a decision descended and made itself.

It was March 15, 2013, eight days after Ken's fifty-second birthday. For six weeks I had postponed numerous trips—seminars and business trainings I had invested heavily in and wanted to attend. But the decision about life and love loomed unmade, and I knew I could not leave until I was clear. The living room, strewn with empty suitcases and stacks of clothes that I had packed, unpacked, and repacked several times, was a daily reminder of my uncertainty and indecision.

The last of my scheduled events, a fundraiser for a worthwhile cause, was the following day in Los Angeles. I desperately wanted to go. With ticket in hand, I called and made hotel reservations, thankfully scooping up a last-minute cancellation. Then I quickly changed my flight, scheduled to leave in just four hours, to the Saturday morning redeye. As I attempted to tidy the house, earth-shattering sobs sprang forth from my soul with an intensity, pitch, and volume I had never heard before. I was sure my cries would alarm the neighbors and passers-by—but I couldn't stop.

Ken, in the midst of launching a new business, walked through the front door as the evening news wrapped up. We exchanged pleasantries and played another verbal ping-pong game of thoughts and feelings. This one ended, uncharacteristically, in an unspoken tie with a palpable sense of mutual defeat. Exhausted, we wearily crawled into bed just before midnight. As I lay next to this kindhearted man who had loved me the best he could, I was paradoxically comforted by his presence, yet felt a distance as strangers passing, eyes averted, on a busy city street. I set the alarm clock for 5:00 a.m. and set my intention to know by morning whether to stay or to go.

I woke naturally at 4:45 and lay in bed starring at the almond-colored plaster ceiling. I asked for a clear answer. I asked for my truth. Three questions effortlessly entered my mind and answered themselves without hesitation.

"Would I go to the fundraiser if it wasn't with Ken?" A resounding "Yes" replied from deep within my being.

"Would I go if money were not an issue?" Again, a strong and solid "Yes."

"Would I go if I lived in LA and didn't have to deal with airline, hotel, and car rentals?" "Yes. Absolutely, Yes."

In a matter of minutes, what had seemed like an eternity of confusion and internal conflict gave way to clarity and peace amid an engulfing wake of loss. I knew I had to leave. Not only was I to go on this trip, but also I finally knew that it was time to venture forth on my own despite the gaping hole that took up residence in my chest. Even as pangs of fear and uncertainty washed over my fragile soul, I knew that I must stand in my truth. With no time to spare or contemplate what I felt, I tried on outfits suitable for a black-tie affair and feverishly packed, tossing knits and shoes and shiny accessories into my carry on bag. Ken watched with sad, knowing eyes, yet found it in his heart, as he always had, to help me get out of the door and get to the airport on time.

In the end, it was more my decision to separate than Ken's. Yet with some obvious reluctance, he let me know that he could never be happy if I wasn't. And it was evident to all that I definitely was not happy. There in the middle of the living room, as the morning sun warmed the carpet beneath our feet, we held each other as streams of tears stained our shirts and black mascara made not-so-graceful tracks down my face. Then—with respect, gratitude, and a love that cannot be measured—we looked thoughtfully into each other's eyes, silently honoring the life that we had shared while knowing we were no longer to be together. It was bittersweet—just like the dark chocolate I have with my coffee each morning.

As I write this, the wind chimes I brought from our garden sing a familiar, melodic song and the three-tiered stone fountain, a special birthday gift from Ken, splashes with the sound of days gone by, the sparkling purity of the moment and the pregnant promise of tomorrow. And I notice a stream of thoughts that arise and call into question my decision. Thunder booms as the birds warn of an impending storm and The Endless Salty Rain begins again. I wonder if it will ever end? I wonder how life would be if I had stayed? I wonder if I could have opened my heart more fully and more deeply honored the wonderful man I was blessed to be with? I wonder if many of the challenges of the past eighteen months—including several moves, the death of my beloved cat, financial ruin and impending bankruptcy, career uncertainty, and a car-totaling rollover accident where I was miraculously unscathed—could have been averted if I had stayed. I wonder . . .

Truth is a moment-to-moment experience based on our presence and perception. And though my mind periodically plays with scenarios of What If? and I question my decision to leave the man I loved so dearly and planned to spend my life with—it *was* my truth at the time. I have come to know that despite our best intentions and plans, we can never know exactly where our choices will lead us. What we can know is that wherever we land, we are always home when we stand in our truth and live in integrity at the ever-present, unchanging zip code of the heart.

Chapter 21

I chose me

by Jo-Ellen Marks

Sunday, November 2, 2008, started out as a spectacular fall day. The sun was beaming, warming the fall breeze as crisp leaves danced about the ground. It was a perfect day to go for a run by the river before the four o'clock Eagles game started. I was so relieved to finally be able to run again after experiencing two back-to-back car accidents six weeks previously. I woke up feeling good after my short run the day before, free of the neck pain and headaches I had experienced after being T-boned in an intersection.

The second accident was minor in comparison, but shocking nonetheless. I had not been in a fender bender of any kind for more than ten years, so imagine my shock just eighteen hours after the first accident when a motorcycle lost control and slammed into my passenger side panel, then flew end over end and landed in front of my car. How was this even possible: two accidents in two days, in my new car purchased just eighteen days ago?

Who would have guessed I was about to be involved in a third, more serious, accident in such a short period of time? I had no idea what was about to hit me as I approached the stop sign on my way to buy a new pair of running shoes, and it was about to make the biggest impact, not only on my car, but on my entire life.

The third accident with a bus on that beautiful Sunday in November was the most severe and left me with a permanent brain injury that still affects my vision to this day. Yet I wouldn't trade in what I learned after these accidents. Yes, if I could have been spared the journey, I would have, but the wisdom I gained over the five years following the accident was a blessing in disguise. Ironically, each accident involved a STOP sign and an intersection, a symbolism that is not lost on me now.

Judging from my physical appearance, or the state of my car after the accident, you wouldn't have drawn the conclusion that I was left with a life-altering injury that would continue to impact me to this day. You see, I see two of you all the time. Yes, two of you—crystal clear images, one overlapping and slightly larger than the other. The official name of this double vision is chronic bilateral monocular diplopia. And the closer you are to me the greater the visual disturbance.

The worst part of my mTBI was the recurring bouts of vertigo I was experiencing. My episodes of vertigo were pretty severe. They felt as if I was drunk *and* hungover at the exact same time: spinning, nausea, headaches, and confusion were the norms. If I felt the symptoms, I had no choice but to lie down, flat on my back, until it passed. As if that wasn't stressful enough, I never knew how long the symptoms would last. Sometimes they lasted two days and sometimes two weeks, and there was no way for me to know or anticipate the duration of each occurrence. I would feel completely helpless as I waited out the pain. Imagine being dizzy, nauseous, confused, in pain, seeing double, and lying flat on your back for an indefinite period of time—two three or four times a month—over the course of almost four years. The doctors were baffled and could not find an explanation of why I was experiencing these symptoms.

My life stopped. Over and over I would have to cancel clients because I couldn't work. I was self-employed and had no disability insurance, so I would push myself to work because I had to. I would often have to cancel plans with friends and family due to being bedridden.

So why would I claim that God blessed me with a brain injury? Because looking back I can see it was part of a plan.

I learned a great deal over those four years of prolonged bouts of vertigo. Prior to my car accidents, I had been through a devastating divorce—the type of divorce movies are written about. Imagine learning that you were getting a divorce after a dear friend walked up to you and said, "I'm so sorry to hear about your divorce."

What divorce?" was all I could mumble back to her.

That's how I found out my marriage was ending. Until that moment I believed I was in a wonderful, loving, committed relationship. I knew he was going through a personally challenging time, but I never imagined he was out there living a complete double life, including treating women to dinner and flowers on my credit card, putting down a six thousand dollar deposit on a car with my credit card, and telling our friends we were getting a divorce. Already in disbelief and shock from learning of my impending divorce, I confronted my husband about the details, asking when he was going to let me in on this little secret. These questions lead to an interaction at our home that was so frightening I barricaded myself in and changed the locks first thing in the morning. My entire world had shattered in a span of fewer than twenty-four hours.

My world continued to unravel in the wake of these events. I was tying up the details of my divorce, selling my home, moving into an apartment, and trying to jumpstart my starving business in the wake of 9/11, but the worst was right over the horizon. Without any warning, my mother passed away that January. I believe I would have healed much faster from my divorce if my Mom had not been taken away so suddenly and unexpectedly. She was my rock. She was the person I called when I needed to talk and cry, and now, suddenly, she was gone. Everything I knew in my life, everything I trusted to feel safe and protected, and everything I felt as though I could believe in was shattered.

Everything stopped. My entire life came to a halt.

I was in pain, not working, single, gaining weight, and alone in my house for endless periods of time. The most challenging aspect of the mTBI continued to be the vertigo. To say this was one of the darkest periods of my life would be a cliché, because it was, but when I look back I can now see that this was the period where my life was being defined. Yes, it was dark, but looking back I now choose to see the pain was part of a bigger plan. I was suffering, but I knew I couldn't stop believing it was going to get better. I began my "bargain" with God.

My bargain was very simple: I promised to not lose faith. I promised to trust and believe that everything God was giving to me was not to punish me; instead I chose to start being grateful for everything I was experiencing, believing that they were blessings, gifts from God hidden in the pain and chaos. I promised God I would continue to uphold my end of the bargain and prayed he would help me find relief from my pain. I chose to start saying "Thank you" for *everything*: Thank you for my ex-husband exactly as he was and exactly as he was not. Thank you for my accidents and where I was as a result. Thank you for my pain, for my financial situation, for my life. I chose it all and said over and over: Thank you God, thank you. Thank you God, thank you. Thank you God, thank you.

I chose to take a different approach whenever I felt I was at the lowest levels of my life. I used my "lying time" as learning time. I stopped listening to the news and music in the morning. Instead as I showered and began my day, I was listening to audiobooks and lectures. I avoided any outside information that reminded me of my injury or outside negativity, choosing to focus on nurturing my mind and healing from the inside out. And then I began to write. It started small with a journal to help me release painful thoughts, developing solutions to help clear my mind and heal both physically and mentally. I had begun writing my own story, capturing what I had experienced, the lessons I had learned, and where I had failed, as well as what I had triumphed over since my divorce.

The days of being bedridden turned out to be a time of great blessing for me. That situation allowed me to spend time listening to amazing teachers on audio and video. Those teachers offered me the wisdom and insight to see where I was selling myself short in all areas of life, where I could be responsible for my actions, and where I had not honored my inner voice. I could see where I had ignored my instincts that had been telling me I was accepting less than I wanted in life. But the universe was about to literally smack me into my humanity and show me how far I had fallen in my self-esteem and worthiness.

As I continued my practice of gratitude, I started to unravel and understand my mental demons. My thoughts of never being good enough, never being thin enough, and never feeling lovable or desirable enough had been ruling my life and clouding my judgment. I could see where I had been selling out on my greatness and accepting less than I was worth. I could see clearly that I had been allowing bad behaviors from the men I was dating because of my fear of being rejected and abandoned again. I was not speaking up for myself, defending my feelings and desires, or sharing what I didn't like about a relationship (if you can even call what I was creating a relationship). I had unknowingly been enabling all of the bad behaviors. I could suddenly see it was me—I had done it. I had been a willing follower, simply out of my need for someone else to define me as lovable, desirable, and worthy as a good partner. There is a sad irony when I realized that the one thing I wanted, love, was continually eluding me, and my worst fears would come true every time, leaving me devastated and heartbroken, and even more desperate to find my mirror of love.

If I had not chosen to practice gratitude, I am unsure how long I would have been struggling in this quagmire of pain. Through gratitude I could see my mirror of love: God was blessing me with each and every failed relationship so I could discover that the only one I needed to receive love from was me. I was the reflection I had been seeking so long. If it had not been for my divorce and car accidents, I may have never discovered the beauty, joy, and love already inside of me.

So I like to think that God blessed me with a brain injury. I have no hesitation to say that the entire sequence of events after that first car accident was anything short of God attempting to get my attention and let me know he was there listening to me at every turn. I had been the one to lose faith in my journey, losing myself along the way. After the third accident, I used to joke that God had my attention, because after sending a car, a motorcycle, and then a bus, I did not want to know what else he had in store for me if I were not willing to stop and listen. Each accident involved a STOP sign at an intersection, and the irony of that simple symbol is still with me until today.

My brain has been healing beautifully. If it were not for that bus on that beautiful day in November, I may have never slowed down long enough to discover how much power and freedom were available in my thoughts. I had the power to heal, I had the power to forgive, and I had the power to love again; they were just hidden inside, like a diamond covered in the mud. Thank you Lord for allowing me to rub away the dirt that was hiding my greatness. Thank you God. Thank you.

Chapter 22

Coming back to joy

by Sally Stap

When I was diagnosed with a brain tumor, my first reaction was to get rid of it. A major medical event was not in my plans, and I was determined to continue my life with a minimal break.

I was a fifty-one-year-old woman with an empty nest enjoying a career as a consultant assisting companies with their information technology spending decisions. I enjoyed traveling and working with different types of companies, which brought my skills together from more than twenty years in computer science. I felt needed, and I believed that I was adding value through my guidance and coaching.

After my diagnosis, I quickly researched options and was ready to discuss three treatments I had uncovered with my neurosurgeon. I could watch and monitor the tumor growth, have radiation, or have it surgically removed. Within two sentences of meeting him, however, I learned surgery was my only option due to the tumor size, location, and side effects I was experiencing. Our discussion was limited to how soon to operate, what to expect, and realistic projections, despite my attempts to minimize the impact on my life. The only good news—the tumor was benign, so I was expected to live. Surgery was scheduled for four weeks later.

I joked, denied, and marched toward surgery with hopes of minimal impact. I assumed the aftereffects I read about would not happen to me. I prayed the surgeon's predictions would be wrong about headaches, hearing loss, and facial paralysis.

However, easy was not my outcome. After nine hours of brain surgery to remove an acoustic neuroma brain tumor the size of a ping pong ball, I became deaf in my right ear, paralyzed on the right side of my face, and immobilized by head pain. When the head pain continued for three, six, and then nine months, I had to acknowledge that returning to my old life was no longer an option.

I was disabled, forced to give up a career I loved. Instead of leading meetings in a corporate setting, I was at home and alone. I started my day with pain pills. A heating pad was my constant companion. Lubricating teardrops replaced natural tears in my right eye, while tears fell from my left one until it was dry, making my head hurt more. The ongoing beat of my heart betrayed the pain in my soul and tightness in my chest. I was adrift, suspended between two worlds. The distance between where I was and where I wanted to be was farther than I could grasp.

When I told myself to overcome and dig deep for energy, I was quickly knocked down by pain. When I ventured into the world, I'd return home in tears and pain after awkward encounters. Those who knew me were incredibly supportive, but after years of independence and self-reliance, it was a struggle for me to accept help. Family smiled while treading softly. Their steady love pulled me along.

The consistency of friendships gave respite from the fog surrounding me.

I hit a wall. Discouraged and exhausted, my body was immobilized by indescribable pain. Crooked smiles were few and far between. Grief and sadness settled in as unwelcome, steady companions. With no hope, happiness, or joy, I found myself limping through an empty life without a drop of contentment. Not living while alive, thrust into the unknown, and forced into unwanted chaos—this was my new existence.

Desiring to experience joy and to live pain free, I took many futile actions to find answers to my puzzling pain. I sought joy but no longer knew peace. I prayed for focus, wisdom, and answers. I heard nothing and felt despair while craving wholeness. I was stuck.

Like a turtle on its back, legs flailing, I had to right myself. My instinct for normalcy and purpose drove me to get upright again. Wanting to use this experience to help others, I myself didn't know how. I needed focus and goals and a new path.

My writing started randomly as a blog to keep family and friends updated through my medical crisis. Eventually blog updates faded away as my topics dwindled down from daily hospital updates to "Well, my head still hurts today."

I looked at my blog contents and pondered how it would read as a book. I put it on a virtual shelf in my computer. The writing was not worthless enough to delete, but not ready to be mined for lessons learned. Who would read such a dismal story?

I enjoyed writing about life. It was a luxury in which I had never before had the time to indulge. Writing fit between the despair of pain and brief spurts of energy. Part or all of my days were spent flat on the couch in pain, but for brief moments, here and there, I was able to escape my present by writing. I had no other purpose than to hone the skill of writing and find a way to occupy my days.

I wrote about pets, motherhood, and my quest for answers. Words captured my reality of living in pain and the emotional agony of facial paralysis. It was cathartic to share some of my struggles with single-sided deafness. With a new understanding and appreciation for perseverance, I tried to give words to the strength required to interact with the world. I marveled at the beauty of people I encountered, I opened my soul, and I wrote vulnerably.

Through my writing, I realized that my preconceived notions about life, love, and friendship were wrong. Forever doesn't exist in this world despite our clinging to the idea with white knuckles. Mirrors reflected intense loneliness as I stared into myself. At some point, self-pity and grief diminished, and I began to navigate the unexpected. As joy began to grow again in my heart, I hardly recognized it; it was so unfamiliar. Guilty flutters were familiar feelings as I recognized my second chance at life while complaining about still being alive. Yet life began to fill again with smiles that were drops in my dry wells. Life began to feel right again.

I was drawn to those who understood that life is for living and not wasting. Due to life's circumstance, I forged new friendships that fit and felt right. I found camaraderie with those who persevere. Together we shared a tenacity to drive forward and embrace new lives. Friendships, beautiful as courageous tulips, broke through the earth, fought to sprout, grow, and eventually bloom, forming a precious bouquet of color. I forged new friendships around the common thread of lost opportunity, as friendships bound by ambition and career faded.

I started to live again and embrace friendships, as unfamiliar happiness overtook grief with increasing frequency. I started to live again with a drop of laughter, a drip of genuine fun, followed by a new comfort with living. Life, not as I lived it, not as I dreamed it, but life with a new angle and view. Living new experiences, each precious in unique ways, I learned to embrace the beginning of a new life page by page. Starting out blank and daunting, each new page is sketched and filled with contentment that is deep and refreshing. I've continued to write and hone my skills for capturing life in words.

Though it felt awkward, I started to share my writing with people. I pulled the files off my computer and compiled a book, which combined my blog with narrative. Today's insights blended with the immediacy of each moment captured in my blog. Time had allowed me to pull back to see that I had learned lessons and grown in positive ways from the experience. By attending writers' conferences and joining a local writing critique group, I embraced myself as a writer and connected with a new me. My new life slowly began to fit like a good pair of jeans conditioned to give at the right places and hug at others.

Somehow, one bit at a time, I came back to life. One word at a time, my book was written. One post at a time, I shared my life and experiences with a community of amazing people. One prayer at a time, I'm rebuilding my faith. One day at a time, I'm finding joy.

Looking back, I recognize how far I've come since brain

surgery. I still have frustrating and painful times, but now I pause and rest. I think about lost dreams that made room for new ones. While many people lose dreams in life, the happiest are those who find new passion and let go of losses. In hindsight, disappointment evolves into a new perspective about the importance of one lost dream while many others remain achievable. Countless other people lose their dream, become entangled in pain, and fail to move forward.

Accepting unwanted change is sticky and gooey. Anyone who has had success abruptly taken away is left shaken and experiences upheaval for a period of time. Every day I wake in the morning and lie still, analyzing my options. Will I wallow here where I am or move forward to seek an achievable goal for this specific day? Breaking down obstacles allows me to find joy in each step toward a new dream.

On my "down" pajama days, lying horizontal, staring out the window:

- I allow the loss of one dream to loom over new dreams and recent accomplishments.
- I exaggerate to myself how lost and alone I am in this monstrous world.
- I chafe at not being able to control everything in my life.
- I compare myself and my life's circumstances to others, minimizing the blessings and goodness that I have experienced.
- I detest being on a need-to-know basis with God.

On "good" days, I'm more balanced:

- I allow myself time to regenerate if needed. I sleep a little more, read a book, or spend time in thought without allowing guilt for misusing time.

- I let my disappointment go, even if for a moment. Life is a series of days we must live.
- I remember that each day takes us somewhere, and some will be better than others. Even if we are still, each day takes us forward.
- I think about God. Not how I fall short in actions, but, quite simply, how big he is even while guiding my life.
- I focus on others. How can I reach out to someone? What can I write to brighten someone's day?
- I accept that when I need to know, I will know.

I've learned to recognize the value in the nature of a safe cocoon and how protection is provided for developing and growing delicate wings. I see how God puts us in a cocoon, kept from knowledge at times and surrounded by a hedge of protection until our wings are stronger than we thought possible.

I've lived an interesting journey, transitioning from a left-brained computer science world with call centers, system implementations, and service level agreements to the world of right-brain art. Touching someone's day by writing a paragraph is now as rewarding as achieving a corporate objective. I recognize the importance of adding value to the world in spiritual rather than commercial ways. If I hadn't experienced downward spirals in my life, mixed with incredible upward ones, I wouldn't be who I am or appreciate today's dream. I wouldn't wonder who I am yet to be.

Chapter 23

I saw the sign

by Bobbi Govanus

It was the summer of 1995. I had left my retail career with Circuit City after putting in sixty hours over the four-day Memorial Day weekend only to have my district manager come in on Tuesday morning berating my staff for not achieving their "Performance Guarantee" quota. I submitted my resignation, and he accepted it and gave me a two-months severance package. He had never been comfortable managing one of the only women managers in the entire chain. As it turned out, he was demoted for losing me since the company was trying to find a way to appeal to the women's market, but that, as they say, is another story.

I spent the first few weeks fending offers from other retailers who were excited that I was now available to come manage their stores. Having had a long (nearly thirty years) and distinguished career with the likes of JCPenney, Sears, and smaller women's clothing stores as district manager and buyer, and, believe it or not, was even a stockbroker, I had literally sold everything from socks to stocks. I was dragging my feet though and had a niggling thought that I was ready to start my own business. I had always treated my career with ownership of my department or store, but I wanted to really be responsible only to myself—no one looking over my shoulder or "managing" me. I worked at a business plan and went on interviews trying to decide what I would do with the rest of my life.

There was one retailer moving to the Minneapolis/Saint Paul market. They had been persistent in staying in contact, and their vice president was flying in to meet me and a few other candidates. They were impressed with the fact that I had opened up the Circuit City stores in Best Buy's hometown with record-breaking sales numbers, twice the original volume projections. The recruiter gave me the hotel name and address at the intersection of Highways 55 and 494. For those of you not familiar with the highways in and around Minneapolis/Saint Paul, Interstate 494 is a big circle surrounding the Twin Cities, and Highway 55 cuts through on its way farther north. Because I lived south and west, I assumed that the hotel was at the intersection nearest me.

I drove to the interview, and as I drew near the intersection I did not see a hotel—I was on the exact opposite end of town. This was before cell phones, so I got off the highway to call and explain my faux pas and reschedule my meeting. As I drove onto the access road to go into the service station, there was a huge sign that said: "Start Your Own Business! TODAY!" It stopped me dead in my tracks. I sat looking long and hard at this sign!

I walked into the gas station and called the recruiter to explain what had happened and apologize. I said I would not be rescheduling as I had decided to go a different career path. The rest, as they say, is history.

I drove home and completed the business plan for my company, For Your Instructors, or FYI, Inc., as it would come to be called. It would be a brokerage service for certified computer trainers who were great at teaching technical stuff but terrible at marketing themselves. It was also a service for education centers that needed a one-stop shop to locate hard to find specialties. I had always been great at numbers (math major in college) and did what I thought were very realistic financial forecasts. I went to four large business banks and was turned down by four male business bankers who thought my million dollar first-year revenue projections were too aggressive by a long shot. I decided to approach a local branch of a smaller SBA lender and talk with a woman. She listened politely and called another loan officer into the meeting. They told me they would be back to me within a week, and within forty-eight hours, my loan was approved.

The first full year my company did $2.5 million in sales, and I hired two employees to help me continue the growth. Eventually, FYI had twelve employees and worked with more than one thousand certified computer trainers throughout the United States and Canada. My trainers taught around the globe.

There really are signs everywhere, but very often they are hidden behind the barrage of media. The billboards may not have the words so clearly spelled out, but I have learned that the most important thing to do is ask for clear direction. Clarity starts with the five rudimentary questions: Who, What, When, How, and the biggie . . . WHY? Each point of my life when I teetered on the precipice of a life decision, I stopped to ask myself these questions and sometimes asked

"Why?" two, three, or even five times to get really clear about my answers. Have you ever been thinking about buying a new car? If you decide on a car model, you will see that car everywhere. If you decide on red, you will see a red car at every stoplight. Are there more Volvos out because you might buy one? No. It is all about your mind being tuned into seeing them.

The sheer focus of making a decision opened my mind to see that sign at a critical point in my life. Six months earlier that same sign would have meant nothing to me. That day it clinched the deal. I am not really someone who jumps into things without a plan. I mull things over and do the Ben Franklin pros vs. cons measuring graph to help me explore all my options. It had served me well up to that point in my life, but because there were too many variables that were unknowns, I could not use that technique successfully to make this life choice.

What I did learn was to trust myself and to trust God to deliver answers. It was and continues to be my responsibility to formulate the questions. Once that became clear, the road took many fewer curves and there were far fewer potholes to get me distracted or disabled on the side of the road.

I find that life has been much more about opening my mind to new possibilities than about conquering them. Once something appears on my radar, I know I can make things work out. Realizing that not making a decision is making a decision, I would literally let someone else decide. There are a million reasons why something "cannot" happen. For example, so many people allow finances to keep them from going for their dream. I heard Stuart Caffey, the founder of Chick-fil-A, say, "If a problem can be solved with money, it is not really a problem." That sunk in and I had to buy in. There are ways to find money, make money, borrow money, or perhaps inherit money. It is a cop-out to blame money for not moving forward.

I have heard and sometimes said, "I am too________." Insert your own word: old, young, uneducated, afraid, shy, average, fat, tall, short . . . and the list could go on for pages and pages. Michael Jordan was cut from his basketball team. But he would not accept that he was too anything but the best. When I stopped putting up barriers, I was able to see and believe that the sign was speaking to me. I could do it!

You have to surround yourself with people who see and recognize who you really are and believe in the person you want to be. It is very hard to have to convince yourself you can succeed when those who constantly put you down surround you. They hold up signs like those taunting put-downs at sporting events: "Strikeout King" or "Choker." You need supporters who hold up signs that tell you "You're # 1!" Fire anyone who does not help you visualize your goal as a reality, not a pipedream.

Beginning with the end in mind will help make the journey much more expeditious. The signs are much easier to recognize when there is a final destination, as it makes it possible to know when you have arrived. I could not live without my GPS telling me nicely to turn here. In life I had been going really fast, making good time in the wrong direction. No Fun. Thank goodness for stop signs that gave me a chance to pause long enough to figure out I was lost.

I was lucky to have seen the sign! It opened up my eyes to my future. I invite you to start looking for those markers along the way to your destiny. You may have been looking, but because you were asking the wrong question—the answer did not make sense. Try asking different questions and put yourself on the right path to achieving your highest purpose.

I've seen the billboard just up ahead with *your* name in lights! I've seen the sign!

part four

BARS: results

Chapter 24

Results

by Nancy Fox

"They eyed one another like game roosters."
Harper Lee *(Go Set a Watchman)*

Results are the benefits received from taking action. Oftentimes results are a hierarchy of achievement, such as the results of a competition in sports or games: first, second, and third place. Comparison to others is a human behavior of judging oneself or group of people against another's skills, qualities, traits, characteristics, abilities, and other measurement categories. Competition is the epitome of results. Does competition have to be the only source of results? No, but many times we feel a result must be monumental, such as an Olympic medal or a World Series or Super Bowl championship. Results are deciding what you want and getting what you want. It is that simple: Benefit—I want to spend time with my dad. Action—I spent time with my dad. Results—I had time with my dad.

Results vary based on desire and level of achievement—what someone wants to happen. Whenever an action is taken, a result or results will occur. Most of us like results that are simple, for example a result of hard work that brought the desired outcome. Sometimes the results are negative or unpleasant. Growing, evolving, and learning from mistakes are essential to progressing cognitively, physically, and spiritually. Results that are not the desired outcome maybe were subconsciously desired because of a belief about self or other reasons that sabotaged the intended outcome.

It is imperative that your head and your heart be aligned in order to get the results you want. Your beliefs must be aligned with your journey. Have you ended up with results that were totally misaligned with your desires? This is a result of a misalignment of your beliefs, desired benefits, and action. You wouldn't drive a car that has the wheels pulling to the centerline of the road would you? The tug of the wheels will pull you towards the oncoming traffic and change your focus. Has this ever happened to you with desires of your heart? You wanted one thing (result), you were distracted by something (took a different action step), and you ended up with the opposite or a different result than you wanted. Hmmm. Is your life the way you designed it, or are you meandering through a misaligned set of beliefs, desired benefits, and actions? Today is the day you align those parts to get the desired benefits and results. The benefits you get will serve yourself and ultimately others.

Are your beliefs and desired outcomes fighting like game roosters? If so, you must get clear on your beliefs. Are your words and thoughts throughout your day, and even in your sleep, telling you that you are not enough or that you are focusing on past situations or events? Are you telling yourself, there is no way this can happen to me because I don't have what it takes to make it happen? Do you believe that no matter what, you will achieve the desired benefits even if it takes longer than you plan for the result to happen? Golf pro Nancy Lopez said, "Do your best, one shot at a time, and then move on." Results happen whether you are in charge, just hanging in there, or along for the ride. Why not design your results?

Take the next steps to design your decision-making and get the results you want.

- Are your results aligned with your beliefs, your desired benefits, and your actions?

- What results have you received from actions taken? Did your beliefs support your desired benefits? Were the results a direct link to your desired benefits? If not, why do you think your results did not meet your desired benefits? Did you take the actions needed to get the desired benefits?

Chapter 25

Decisions built to last

by Debra M. Lewis

Daily decisions we make affect everyone in our environment—they have an impact. Organizations also face daily decisions. Every employee wants to be heard, valued, and supported. A recurring point of stress for employees can be the hiring/promotion process. Who we choose to work closely with is a gift that keeps on giving . . . or not. How well do you handle stress? Are your decisions and actions consistent with your values, beliefs, and intent? Do you see opportunity in every difficulty? How often do you actually end up with what you did not want?

- Ever applied for a new job and were crushed or angered when you didn't get it?
- Ever been thrilled to be the one chosen for an open position or promotion only to find others sabotaging your efforts once in it?

What happened leading up to the decision? In the interview? Afterwards (that night, days, months, years later)?

What would it look like if you could far exceed your

wildest dreams—in your career, your personal relationships, and your future?

Societal pressure: classic "win-lose" or not?

Two people want the same job and are interviewed for it. Does this have to be a classic "win-lose" situation? What are your options? I believe in a concept called Infinite-Win. Friend and CEO Deb Boelkes and I formulated three elements of this mindset: caring, collaborating, and creating.

Imagine how I felt when I shared this alternative approach in personnel selection processes with a former CEO of a multimillion-dollar firm. He strongly argued, "Two people want the same position? You either get the job or not. It's win-lose." He could find no merit to my views. He just wasn't interested.

He could be right, but what if he's not? What must happen to achieve something better? My years of leadership experiences are solid testament that there is something better. Trial-by-fire is a harsh but invaluable method of understanding dynamics and predicting the future.

Magic frequently happens now because of the people with whom I'm blessed to spend time, as the following story illustrates. By changing my perspective, I could see the many tiny decisions leading up to each big one. Personnel selection panels have become a favorite way to promote decisions, which will positively impact organizations. You can make important decisions in five minutes or less. It will be your best gift ever.

"The vote is a tie. It's up to you to decide. Ma'am, what's your decision?"

I leaned back in my chair to consider my options. The

selection panel had quickly narrowed my choices down to two highly qualified people—an inside candidate and an outside candidate. This looked like a classic win-lose scenario: one candidate wins the job and the other one loses. But did it have to be?

I wondered, why the split vote? After much prodding, one panel member who most opposed choosing the inside candidate, cited something she had done many years earlier. On the other hand, another panel member felt the outside candidate knew too little about our organization. *What would you do next?*

After hearing their rationale, I took less than five minutes to make up my mind, finalizing the panel decision with my vote. What I did *next* ensured the decision was implemented as I intended.

I chose to deliver the results of the panel decision myself. I spoke first with the inside candidate, whom I'll refer to as Iris.

> *Me:* Iris, I really want to thank you for putting yourself out there to apply for this important position. I was very pleased with the quality of the candidates who applied, including you. I know you could do this job. I wanted to give you some feedback on the process.
>
> *Iris:* I wanted this job so much. I know I could've done a better interview.
>
> *Me:* If you had been selected, you would've been in for a very tough time because several people who've known you since you started here may not ever give you a break. They remember who you were years ago, not the person I see today.

Iris: I know, Colonel Lewis. I've grown a lot over the years here.

Me: You know how to overcome anyone who doubts your capabilities? By doing one hell of a job. That, I know you can do. Because of what you've shown me, I believe in you and your potential. You've got the job, if you still want it.

Iris: What? Really? I've got the job? Yes! Yes! Yes! *(She burst into tears and gave me a bear hug.)* I want it more than anything. You won't regret this. I promise you.

Next, I delivered the news to the outside candidate, whom I'll refer to as Olivia.

Me: Olivia, I want to thank you for applying for this important position. It's clear you can do this job right now. Our panel was very impressed with your interview. I was in the enviable position of having several highly qualified candidates compete. I see you as a valued member of our USACE family (our overall organization).

There was one area in the interview where you can definitely improve. That made the difference, so unfortunately I won't be offering this job to you today. It had to do with demonstrating a better understanding of how we are organized and our role in the region.

Olivia: Thank you, Colonel Lewis, for your words. I realized in the interview that I needed to do more research about what you do.

> *Me:* I'd really like to help you any way I can. We do have other positions that you could apply for, but I can see how this position really suits you. Did you know we have forty-four other districts in the world with this exact position? They open up frequently.
>
> I would be happy to write a letter of recommendation for you and assist you in identifying resources to better prepare for your next interview. You are that good, and you could make a positive impact on what we do for the nation.
>
> *Olivia:* Thank you for your offer of support. I think that's the nicest notification I've ever received that I didn't get the job.
>
> *Me:* That's because my answer is "not yet," but soon I know you will. Good luck and let me know what I can do for you.

Later that night. What do you think was the focus and follow-up discussion between each candidate and her family or friends? Compare that with what normally happens after filling a vacancy.

One year later. The selection panel member most opposed to the inside candidate paid a personal visit to Iris and told her, "I was wrong. You are perfect for this position."

Eighteen months later. Olivia (the outside candidate) called me to say she had just been selected for the same position in a nearby USACE district command and to thank me again for my support and encouragement. She was very happy.

Two and one-half years later. I received an email from Iris soon after I deployed to my third command of an engineer district, this time in Central Iraq. She wanted me to know that she was in her dream job and could not imagine a better place to be. In fact, the new commander had already approved a promotion for her.

Ten years later. I received a Facebook post prior to Iris's retirement stating, "COL Lewis, thank you from the bottom of my heart for believing in me and giving me a chance to prove that I WAS the right person for the job ten years ago! I absolutely loved my job and felt so blessed to be in such a wonderful position. . . ."

How important was this decision? Being fairly new myself, I knew the stakes were high. The better the decision, the more the command (and I) benefited directly. The executive assistant position supported my entire engineer organization responsible for a four-state area with 850 employees and nearly a half-billion-dollar budget.

I enjoy setting in motion positive outcomes. The above example is only one of thousands of personnel decisions I made in my career.

Some essential elements

It may take a minute, five minutes, or an hour to make each decision in your day. With certain shortcuts, the risk increases. After learning how to integrate the elements below into my decision-making, I identify inconsistencies and consider opposing views. This approach leads to better decisions affecting not only today, but causing ripple effects in the future.

Goal. *What is your desired goal or outcome?* Even when shared, others may perceive the situation differently than you think they do.

Philosophy. *Why is the goal important?* Your philosophy explains the larger context of why your actions and questions make sense to others.

Assumptions. *What key assumptions are needed for a decision to make sense or trigger a review should the situation change?* As a word of caution, other people often present assumptions as fact.

Facts. *What unshakeable facts impact or force decisions right now?* Few facts withstand the test of time. Beliefs, while strongly held, are not facts.

Criteria/Standards. *What makes one option better than another?* Consider criteria or standards that might eliminate an option from consideration.

Strategies. *What strategies achieve the desired outcome?* Identify specific strategies to ensure a desired outcome. Too often people confuse action with progress.

Helpful tools, insights, and experiences

Based on my training and experiences, I have identified some tools that you can use in your decision-making.

The ultimate empowerment tool: effective questions. Effective inquiry is the most powerful tool I learned outside the classroom, and I was taught by the best. Doug Krug is an enlightened leader, friend, and talented author/consultant. Within hours of arrival, Doug can transform a room of people who hate each other into a collegial body working closely together. How? When we ask better questions of others and ourselves, decisions become obvious. Additionally, relationships improve. Every so often, though, tough decisions must be made and that takes courage.

Instant decisions are risky. Beware of immediate, knee-jerk responses. Rarely do they consider the essential elements of decision-making.

After graduating from Harvard Business School, I taught problem-solving for three years at West Point. Research tells us that instant decisions lead to suboptimal outcomes, and that can lead to more problems than you start with. Indeed, the chance of getting exactly what you don't want is dramatically increased.

Neutralize the tyranny of yes-no people. Ever had someone publicly shout, "Yes" or "No" to force an immediate answer? I learned the hard way that caving into pressure rarely leads to a better decision. Once you agree with the question and/or situation, the appropriate response is usually somewhere in between.

Amazing people often hide. Bad behavior occurs when emotionally charged trigger words are used—sometimes unknowingly. By acknowledging others' concerns, you may be able to cut through some of the tension without agreeing with opposing positions.

Hone your instincts. My sisters-in-arms and I graduated from West Point (established in 1802) in the first class to include women (1980). Early on, I could see and focus on the bigger picture even when current realities were troubling.

This larger world view grew into a cosmic perspective as I incorporated and began to trust things that cannot be seen or touched, but exist nonetheless. I opened my mind, calling upon all my senses, and let my intuition experience the natural flow of life. This was a new and powerful insight, which I added to theory and accepted practices learned in training. This holistic approach to life and challenges requires mind, body, and spirit.

Stiff resistance or friction to my attempts to head one way never discouraged me. Often it indicated I was meant to do something else or learn something far more important, even if it was painful.

What do you believe? I believe when we honor each other and work closely together, our possibilities expand and the sky is the limit. An avid and continuous learner, I'm always growing and changing. While I know there are those who may be fearful of change, I continue to believe that they too will benefit over time with understanding.

I believe there are answers to every question and solutions to every problem. Options are boundless and frequently closer than you think. I'm fascinated by the experiences and insights of others. Trust is difficult for those who have been burned or discounted. But like Mark Twain, I believe strangers are just friends I haven't met yet. In addition to Infinite-Win, CEO Deb Boelkes and I believe there is a hidden hero in each of us. This is the inner person with whom one chooses to engage.

Look deeper. Ever had someone try to convince you that the decision he or she wants you to make is simple and so obvious? Have you ever tried to separate a fragile necklace from a larger tangle of jewelry? Most decisions you make daily seem easy enough to untangle . . . that is, until you look deeper.

Unless you use special tools to gently separate the jumbled jewelry, you could easily find that the harder you pull, the more firmly entangled it becomes. The ability to see the larger consequences involved in the context of your decisions is invaluable. Keep in mind, even if things are logical, they may never work.

Things are not what you think. Decision-making is often risky and lonely, so find ways to fortify your courage in the face of adversity. Many people are well intentioned, yet misguided with strong opinions. Stay cool, calm, and pleasant. You are more likely to offer a thoughtful response and remain focused on the desired outcome.

Who has your back? True mentors and authentic relationships are rare. When found, they give you room and confidence to maneuver. Even when I'm not able to articulate why I change direction, my spouse, Doug Adams, has always had my back and trusts my choices. He's secure enough within himself and doesn't feel threatened by my initiative.

Seek feedback and engagement. Continuous engagement and feedback serve to mitigate or to avoid possible pitfalls, while encouraging opportunities.

This point was emphasized whenever my students performed a simple exercise. With backs toward each other and each group holding seven puzzle pieces, one student gave instructions to the other, while her/his partner was silent. In one hundred times, only one team successfully put the pieces together.

Feedback and constant engagement are that important.

Closing thoughts

Laura Steward, gifted author and friend, recently interviewed me for her show, "It's All About the Questions." She asked me to list my top three leadership lessons based on my experiences. My answer? "People, People, People." Despite facing significant adversity, I have thrived and learned to create the world I want through my decisions. How much better can you make your life? See what happens when you apply a lifetime of experience to every decision you make.

I believe in you. Create the world and the life YOU want.

Chapter 26

Sound decision

by Melinda Cooper

The moment you see the change coming in your life you begin to understand the feeling. The moment comes when you know something is changing—it could be your feelings; it could be your thoughts running through your mind; or, finally, it is your heart calling for help from the inside out. Yes, you remember something took you to that point. I've learned through my life that change comes only when something becomes so unbearable you don't have any choice except change. Another option is that someone else brought the change into your life for a greater purpose, which of course you don't realize what it is at that one moment. Life prevails exactly as it leads you into the greater life. Change is constant, and accepting it takes strength and courage.

My day came the moment my mother and I realized there was not going to be healing for her cancer. We faced the reality that the battle had already been decided; now we were simply going to walk through the steps that were in front of us. So we began our journey; we talked, walked, and cried through each step knowing the inevitable was coming, and we were picking up speed to the finish line. Gratefully we both understood without speaking a word; we both knew our walk that we had decided to be on together side-by-side. As the days went forward, the time seemed to pick up speed without any mercy.

Each day, as we were going through our necessary change that life had brought to us, it was a bumpy ride. We were experiencing the moments that would linger through our family's lifetime. Medicine, discussion, rest, medicine, bathing, and finally sleep—the time was running faster than we thought. It was taking us into a speed of life, changing per the minutes rather than the days. We both knew this was marking time at a pace that would eventually take us over. We woke to the new day with prayer and then onward to the daily process of medicine, discussion, rest, medicine, bathing, and finally sleep into the night once again. Yes, we walked through the emotions of knowing what she would not be able to physically see or to experience—those things she had always dreamed to be a very large part of her life.

Our walk took us to prevailing and learning the meaning of life within our home, for I would not place her into a nursing home. I would not allow anyone to place her on machines. We had agreed it would be in God's hands, and we would walk the path together. As the walk picked up speed we knew the answers; we had accepted God's path for us; and we accepted the change without fight, without fear of how to battle such a moment. Life was directly in front of us. Peace was coming and one day would indeed take her into the next level, leaving me behind, leaving our family to grow from the change.

The day finally arrived, and God gave mercy to my mother and placed her in his home with love, peace, and no pain. Within a moment my mother won her ride home, and I won my ride to peace and calm—she passed away in her sleep. I knew the battle we had experienced as warriors together for the last twelve years was over. We fought the best fight we had at the beginning—doctors, second opinions, radiation, and chemo treatments. On and on we tried them all. Now it was all over, and change was in front of me once again. It would be something new and something different, living again a life that was focused on my children, my husband, and my family.

I knew in my heart life had changed in so many ways and in various movements. I knew the view of the world that I had prior to my mother's illness changed faster than I had ever imagined. It was a change of a greater reality, one that had changed me for my entire life. Change comes in so many ways; it brings us to evaluate the meaning of our own lives. Are we walking in a direction that will echo far beyond us? Or are we living in the moment that screams change within each moment? This long journey had indeed brought out its own destiny and discoveries. It brought a reality of life that I had never thought I would know by the time I was forty. Yet here it was looking me in the face. So, quickly I returned to work attempting to focus and get back into the game of my life. I was eager to make a new kind of mark, one that would leave a memory of positive, fluid action for others to receive benefits from.

I had decided that instant, which had been coming for such a long time, that life was too precious to waste on a fast-paced nothingness going to nowhere. The days became difficult as I watched people maneuvering into positions of what they believed would enhance their power. I now was spending my days listening to the word that flowed from other people, meaning nothing further than rhetoric of their own importance. Yes, life and the battle my mother and I had just experienced had indeed changed me. So I began making my adjustments. I was ready to get back into the swing of things of what I had once called a normal life. I found myself wanting to understand why so many people had placed their thoughts on being "very important" and why they had forgotten they were "average people" doing very important jobs.

I watched as they each would create momentum to push forward without worrying how their steps forward were crushing those they stepped on to get to their targets. I listened as they laughed over their conquests without looking backward at what had been left as remains. Yes, I know I had changed, and I was quickly wondering what I was going to now create for me. I definitely knew a new meaning of my life, and I understood what I was contemplating as my next best step. Then change came to me yet again.

It was a Friday evening at seven o'clock when my father suddenly passed away from a heart attack. I felt it in my heart; I knew to reach out to him prior to that fatal call from the hospital asking me to get there as quickly as I could. I knew simply by the voice of the nurse who had placed the call my father was gone. It hit me like a ton of bricks. Not only had my mother gone to heaven just a few short years ago, now my father was gone, and it was another major change in my life and the life of our entire family. Change—here it was in front of me; this time it came suddenly; it was bold, and obviously it was being brought to me.

It took only two weeks after my father's passing that I knew what I was going to have to do. I came home to let my husband, who had been with me throughout the entire ordeal, know that I no longer was interested in my job or in the office where I was working, and I couldn't work any longer in the position I held. I knew in my heart that I was not where I was meant to be. We made our plan of attack, and we were declaring our next change!

The office would be silent and no one else should be there to run into on this my special day. It was Saturday, January 3, 2009, when I left the agency I had been with for more than eighteen years. I called one of my dearest of friends who joined me; we had worked together for fifteen of those years, so she completely understood. We had talked about it since October 2008 just after my father's passing. She knew and was ready to help me out. We cleaned my desk, we secured my "official files," and we delivered and put away all that was needed. We cleaned the furniture; we set my voice-mail and finally sent out the email stating I was gone.

The moment came flashing with excitement and a relief all at once. I knew this change was on my heart and presenting an opportunity to grow at my own rate. I knew it was time for me to make a difference in a different way and definitely within a different manner. There isn't anything greater than your heart singing from deep within you when the decision you make is correct. Life's meaning had changed for me!

Chapter 27

Healing pain from the inside out

by Marissa O'Neil

Life is comprised of a myriad of experiences or "dots" as Steve Jobs described them. When threaded together, and with the benefit of hindsight and reflection, they reveal our heartfelt purpose in life. Some experiences confuse and distract us from our desired path, while others align us with our gifts and talents to accelerate us forward. It is my belief that there are signs along our journey of life that, if recognized, help us to navigate the uncharted waters of our lives. The essential question is: Are you awake and listening?

Several years ago, I found myself adrift from my consciously intended path. Interestingly and consequently, my body physically shut down. I was not paying attention to the subtle signs of unhappiness in my professional or personal life. Thus, my body created symptomatic physical pain, a sign I could not ignore, to seize my attention and generate an awareness that something in my life was off balance and needed to change.

In an attempt to escape from a life I no longer loved, I went on a weekend ski trip to Mammoth Mountain in

California with a group of friends. During my first run of the day, a snowboarder sideswiped me from behind causing a tangled crash. I landed on my back with my skis still attached to my bindings and my legs forming an acutely twisted X. I jumped up quickly, ignored the twinges in both knees, and skied the rest of the day.

At the time, I was unaware that the pain from the fall was an important sign I needed to acknowledge, accept, and integrate the lesson being presented to me.

After the ski lifts closed for the day, we gathered for dinner at a Mexican restaurant at the base of the mountain. When it was time to walk back to the lodge, I attempted to stand up and realized I could not move my legs. My mind flashed back to the fall and sharp twists my legs were in eight hours earlier. My left knee felt like someone cut it open and tied all the muscles in a tight knot.

After limping and being carried back to the condo, I took 800 milligrams of ibuprofen to reduce the inflammation and started the traditional medical treatment of an acute injury: Rest, Ice, Compress, and Elevate (RICE).

As a certified strength and conditioning specialist, I knew that proper treatment in the first seventy-two hours following a serious injury is vital to a quick recovery. So I kept my knee elevated and iced throughout the night, hoping the pain and swelling would diminish by morning. Unfortunately, that was not the case. As I sat up in bed, it was clear the pain was substantially greater than the night before. My knee joint had stiffened from a lack of lubrication during the night and was extremely painful to bend or straighten. I hobbled into the kitchen where my friends were talking excitedly about which ski run they were planning to conquer first that day. Staggering past them I headed straight for the couch to continue icing and elevating my knee, fighting back tears and wondering why they could all go out and have fun while I had to remain inside suffering from this excruciating pain.

As my friends changed into their ski attire and trickled out of the cabin towards the slopes, Amy, a spiritual friend, stayed back to clean the condominium before we checked out. She always encouraged me to explore a deeper meaning and purpose in life by asking better questions and learning how to shift the energy. Up to this point I had resisted the suggestion, however, faced with the current crisis, I was eager to try anything to release the pain.

I asked Amy her thoughts about my knee injury. She explained Louise Hay's perspective about how every body part parallels and signifies an aspect of one's present life. On a symbolic level, the injured knee represented a major change in my life and my inability to bend or flow with the new direction my life was taking. So Amy asked me, "What are you resisting giving in to?" This question, and what was about to unfold, became a pivotal moment in my life.

In this moment of reflection, I saw a correlation between my knee pain and the wellness company I worked for, which had just announced a substantial strategy shift. Addressing Amy's question, illustrated by my knee pain, gave me the space, awareness, and insight to re-examine my life in a new light and led to an opportunity to create positive change for my future. Clearly I did not want to continue the journey with my employer.

So I asked myself, "If I can do anything, what did I dream of doing?"

Since the age of seventeen, I envisioned an integrative wellness center that fused eastern and western medicine to empower people to heal their mind, body, and spirit from within. With the dramatic strategy shift by my current employer away from a small family culture to a more formal corporate culture, it became clear this was an opportunity to follow my dream of starting my own company. While sitting in a lounge chair with a pen and paper in hand, I brainstormed ideas and next steps on how to establish a new business.

Once this entrepreneurial idea blossomed, the writing flowed effortlessly onto the paper: one page filled, then two, and three. As words emerged, I quickly began to visualize my new business venture and the people who could help me bring this dream to fruition. This vision did not seem daunting or unattainable, as I had previously believed it would be. Once the details were fully conceived, I literally felt the cells in my body shift, almost like they were germinating this new possibility into existence. This was one of the biggest breakthroughs in my life! In this new moment of awareness, I recognized how every moment of my academic and professional training, as well as personal life experiences leading up to this point, were preparations for this opportunity. A smile quickly spread across my face as I surrendered into the excitement of a new path that just emerged.

My friends startled me out of this creative vortex when they returned for lunch. I discussed my breakthrough with them and without thinking about my knee, I stood up to join them in the kitchen and to my amazement, walked over pain free. To this day I am in awe of this experience!

Now I have a much deeper appreciation for the human body and how the subtle, and not so subtle, signs we experience can affirm we are on the right path, trigger a pause, or reorient us back to our purposeful life direction. From that moment on, I dedicated my life to further studying the nuances of body-mind connections and how our body communicates by sending messages that can stimulate awareness in every breath we take. My purpose and mission in life is to help people remove their pain physically, mentally, emotionally, and spiritually so that they can bring into balance that which they may feel is lacking, and thus experience the essence and wholeness of who they really are. In working with clients along these dimensions, they report experiencing deeper levels of self-love, clarity of purpose, and freedom to express their authentic truth.

One of my clients, Tom, is a fifty-eight-year-old carpenter who has had hand and wrist pain for the past five years. His physician diagnosed the condition as arthritis and set out an expectation that it would worsen as he aged. Tom had also seen physical therapists, acupuncturists, and massage therapists to try to relieve his persistent pain.

With five years of intense pain and numbness in his hands, he had nearly given up hope of living pain free. Fortunately, his wife heard about the impact of my work from one of their neighbors and hired me immediately to evaluate and work with her husband. Together, we cocreated an experience where we worked on healing the root causes, and within three sessions he felt pain relief and within eight sessions was pain free. Moreover, he shared that from our work together, he admitted, "For the first time in my life, I feel comfortable in my own skin."

My message to you is: Pay attention to the pain in your life, because it's trying to teach you something you're not aware of yet or have been ignoring. Listen to the subtle signs along your journey and allow your body to be your guide to a greater awareness and insight. You will discover a whole new world opening up for you: deeper connections, greater self-love, and new opportunities aligned with your soul's purpose.

I invite you to reflect on five key elements to understanding the significance of pain. These will initiate an internal dialogue exploring the nature of your pain and provide insight to what your body-mind is experiencing and communicating.

Awareness: Are you currently experiencing pain in your body? Or have you in the past? Where do you feel the pain? What does it feel like? Expand your awareness by connecting with this feeling.

Acknowledgement: Acknowledge and honor your pain. Try talking to your pain with a childlike curiosity. You can say, "I see you, I feel you. Now I want to understand you." Ask, "What are you here to teach me in this moment?" Then listen for how your body-mind communicates with you.

Acceptance: Learn to accept your pain as a friend, an ally. If you just want to get rid of it, you won't learn the lesson your friend (pain) wants to teach you. This is why pain typically comes back in the same place, because the root cause of the pain never healed. Invite your friend (pain) to stay as long as it needs to so you can master the lesson it's here to teach. Maybe ask the pain to stay for a cup of tea and chat. Ask what the pain needs from you without any attachment to the outcome.

Love: Love heals all wounds. Love yourself unconditionally for co-creating the pain. Love your body for bringing you the awareness that something is out of balance in your life. Be grateful for this opportunity to cocreate a new possibility together.

Surrender: Surrender to the pain. Surrender to the outcome. Surrender to the attachment of what it looks like. Surrender to the emergence of a new path or opportunity that your soul is yearning for.

Learning to explore and navigate through these five elements will empower you to consciously choose new thoughts and create new patterns of awareness along your journey. As you cocreate a deeper relationship with your body-mind, you will learn that all the answers lie within. And this is how you heal, from the inside out.

Chapter 28

An ER visit went wrong

by Kyla Dillard

On May 4, 2015, I stopped in to visit a friend. A large dog was barking aggressively at me through the window. My friend's daughter removed the dog from the office, but he continued to bark from behind a French door for about five minutes before he got quiet.

I asked to use a washroom—big mistake. The second the French door was opened, the dog rushed in and grabbed my lower left leg. I was wearing black pants, the dog was black, and the corner of the room was dimly lit. My friend could not see that the dog was actually biting me.

I sternly keep repeating, "Get him off me, get him off me, get him OFF me." My friend is about ninety-five pounds, and the dog looked to be over a hundred pounds. She and her daughter were trying to pull him off. He had his teeth sunk deeply into my leg for at least ten seconds and was nearing the bone, so in a much harsher voice I said, "He is biting my leg and shredding my flesh—get him off!"

The daughter pulled him off, and then he went for my other leg. She got him to release for a second, and I pushed back and bolted through the French door, closing it behind me. The girl said, "It's okay, I've got him." I said, "No. I am not coming through that room, and you are not opening this door. Get that dog away from me and confine it, right now!"

I lifted my bloody pant leg. I could see the large laceration and the subcutaneous fat and muscle beneath it. My friend's daughter said, "Oh, my God!"

With two deep punctures and a major laceration/defect in my leg, I drove myself to the hospital..

A triage nurse saw me within twenty minutes. Her contribution was taking my temperature and blood pressure and putting the cheapest, scratchiest, most likely-to-stick-to-a-wound gauze on the leg so that no one had to see the laceration and punctures. That would have been an excellent time to take the three minutes required to flush the wound to get the bacteria and dog saliva out of it.

I was put back out in the general waiting room. I called my girlfriend and told her I was hurt, which hospital to meet me at, and asked her to bring me some pain medicine. Amanda arrived with the Tylenol®-codeine #3 that had been prescribed for my arthritic knees. Thank God I'd had the presence of mind to call and ask her to bring it because the adrenaline was waning and the injury was becoming more painful.

We talked until my codeine wore off, and I took another dose, realizing that I had been at the ER, with a shredded leg, for more than four hours. I had been offered nothing for pain, not even an ice pack. By now the "golden period" of four hours for wound closure had passed. I called the receptionist for my vet business and asked her to bring me a thirty-milliliter syringe of sterile saline solution with betadine solution.

As a veterinarian for twenty-eight years, it was hard to watch medical incompetence.

Once I had the sterile solution, I went into the bathroom, took off the horribly adhered bandage, and flushed out my own wounds, using the toilet as a waste receptacle for my bloody body fluids. I had no choice but to replace the outer layers of the cheap gauze.

Six hours after the attack, an ER doc came in. Instead of a proper cleanup and surgical prep, the ER doc flushed the wound with about ten milliliters of saline and swabbed the open wounds with a chlorhexidine-soaked plastic applicator, but didn't thoroughly clean the skin surrounding the openings.

He proceeded to do the worst suture job I had ever seen done by a medical professional. It looked like it had been done by a blind drunk who was on a moving streetcar in San Francisco.

I was having more pain than I had had during the attack. I took some photos of the suture job and was able to see that the two puncture wounds on the back of my leg not only had sutures that were way too tight, but the way the needle bites had been taken, the sutures were pulling hard on my skin between the wounds, cutting through my skin at the edges. The front wound had internal tissue peeking out between the sutures.

By noon the next day, I couldn't take the pain. After I saw a few appointments, I had Katie, my tech, surgically prep my leg. The suture lines were horribly inflamed, and my skin was actively being strangulated.

After giving myself a local anesthesia, I ripped out all the offending sutures and cut out the dead tissue, then closed my leg wounds with sterile surgical staples. YouTube links to the video of me performing surgery on my own leg are online.

Turns out, ER docs are not supposed to close dog bite wounds unless they are on the face. I got the correct information by speaking with a dermatologist in Miami after my leg became infected.

Six weeks later, with a horrible infection in the wounds, I went back to the ER and was told that I was rushing things and needed to be patient. A different ER doc gave me another antibiotic script, telling me to leave it dry and uncovered.

My regular doc was horrified when I saw her the next day. She immediately referred me to a wound specialist (three months until the appointment) and set me up with a wound care nurse in the meantime.

The wound care nurse said it would take almost a year for the wounds to heal with specialty bandaging needed three times a week at a cost about forty thousand dollars in home health care charges.

The video of me doing surgery on myself was broadcast on the 11 o'clock evening news, and I was documenting my progress on Facebook. I continued to think it was no big deal until a classmate of mine sent me a picture of his titanium leg and told me to stop screwing around with my injury.

Several elder care nurses who saw it also freaked out and told me I was headed for amputation if I didn't get the eschars debrided.

At seven weeks after the attack, I decided it was time to get serious again and to take matters into my own hands. I wrote a script for medical maggots and had them shipped to Niagara Falls, New York (they are an unapproved drug in Canada where I live), where I put them in my leg.

There is video documentation of the maggots doing the most amazing wound debridement in only five days. My only concern on those days was the health and well-being of my maggots.

The maggots eventually shortened my healing period by at least seven months. If maggots crawl across your skin, it tickles. Inside the wounds, even though they are wriggling constantly, you feel nothing.

The maggots cleared the wound, and I was able to see that one of the deep punctures in the back of the leg was open all the way through to the large laceration on the front of the leg. The dog's canine teeth had touched inside my leg on the covering of the bone.

Due to a cancellation, the wound doctor saw me earlier than planned; it was two months after the attack. In just a week, the maggots had fully debrided the wounds and the wounds were closing well.

The wound doctor told me that healing would be greatly accelerated if the leg were wrapped with a compression bandage to decrease the swelling, but to still expect healing to take nine more months for the wound to fully close.

I didn't like that prediction, so for the third time, I made a decision to do it differently.

I bought a hyperbaric chamber, which massively increases wound healing. I used it daily for two weeks, three times per week.

How does one massively reduce the swelling between muscles in the shortest period of time? Leeches. I purchased twelve leeches at a bait shop nine weeks after the attack. Only one had any work ethic; I went fishing with the others. Bass love them.

Leeches are extremely muscular and are hermaphrodites, so I named him Caitlyn. Caitlyn latched onto my leg and took out approximately twenty milliliters of fluid in the first minute of being attached. My wound nurse was there to witness it. She was impressed. In between feedings, I kept Caitlyn in a sundry jar filled with water on my kitchen table.

I discontinued the compression bandages because they made my legs ache at night and each compression wrap cost two hundred dollars. The wound care nurse told me that she had been doing this for thirty years and her exact words were: "We're doing it wrong." My alternative treatment had been effective.

Eighty-six days from the attack and only forty days after I put maggots in, I was waterproof; my leg had healed beautifully.

Chapter 29

The black cloud

by Diane Watson

My mom always called me the black cloud because natural disasters seemed to follow me. Although I've experienced my fair share of these adventures, I've managed to survive them mostly unscathed. I survived a 6.1 magnitude earthquake in California, the 500-year flood in Houston, and an automobile accident in Miami where I drove through flying cars and raining glass like I was inside a snow globe.

My charmed life came to an unfortunate end when I was forced to face down a formidable foe named Andrew—Hurricane Andrew to be exact. This storm had such an overwhelming impact on South Florida that those who experienced its wrath are still on a first name basis with the storm.

I lived in South Florida for twenty-three years without ever experiencing a hurricane. I always had a healthy respect for Mother Nature, but never anticipated the tempest that was headed my way. Residents who had experienced hurricanes in the past were astonished by the power and destruction of this storm.

On August 21, 1992, we were aware that the first hurricane of the season was lurking in the Caribbean. All of the good residents of South Florida headed out to buy batteries, gas, water, bread, and milk. Liquor stores also did a brisk business. Initially it appeared that the storm might skirt the South Florida coast and make landfall somewhere north of Miami. However, by Sunday night the winds of Hurricane Andrew increased to 170 mph as it decimated the island of Lutheran in the Bahamas. We were in trouble.

My home was situated twelve miles inland from the coast, so a storm surge was not a threat. We were *not* told to evacuate. The house was well built (or so I thought) and had hurricane shutters to cover all of the windows. Five friends from the coast and from the Florida Keys actually evacuated to my house thinking it would be safer.

After midnight we saw our last shocking image of Hurricane Andrew on the television radar. The storm had suddenly taken a sharp left turn and was now on latitude that would take it over Homestead, Florida, and the nuclear power plant. That meant that my home would be in the north eye wall—the area of strongest winds. We had not anticipated that the next seven hours would be a dangerous roller coaster ride, in the dark, with only flashlights in our hands. Then the power went out.

The pressure in the house decreased dramatically, making our heads feel like they would explode. We were relieved when we felt a "pop" that relieved the pressure, but didn't realize that it meant the roof was beginning to separate from the house.

Water began pouring into every room from the ceilings and light fixtures. An interior bathroom that should have been our safe room was now the base of a rushing waterfall. We pulled down shower curtains to cover the beds to protect them from the massive leaks that were multiplying. Photographs and artwork were quickly yanked off the walls and hidden under the dining room table to protect them from destruction.

You often hear hurricane and tornado victims talk about the sound of the wind being similar to a train. During Andrew, I only remember the thundering crash of what sounded like trucks smashing into my house. In reality the sound was caused by large pieces of my neighbors' homes slamming into mine. Our neighborhood originally contained picturesque dwellings with cupolas on every roof. The hurricane ripped these structures off every roof and shot them into any home or car in its path. One of the cupolas smashed into my hurricane shutters and through two bedroom windows. It sounded like a bomb—glass was flying everywhere. Most terrifying: Andrew was now *inside my house!*

For the first time I began to wonder if we would survive.

Suddenly one of my friends screamed and pointed to the kitchen ceiling. In the glow of flashlights it appeared that a black snake was slithering across my ceiling. In reality the ceiling was being pulled apart. For a few terrifying moments, the ceiling shuddered as if it housed a heavy breathing monster. Within seconds a large chunk of ceiling came crashing down on the furniture below.

After that first breath-stopping collapse, we began to move from room to room (like rats in a maze) looking for the next ceiling sections that might crash down on our heads. As they fell, piece-by-piece, wet plaster spread over furniture, the floor, and all my belongings. Every material object I owned was now in ruins.

While we looked for falling ceilings, our flashlights focused on the wall that separated the dining room from the bedroom with the smashed window. It was becoming saturated and in danger of collapsing. We knew if that wall came down the hurricane would ravage the rest of the house. Two of us pushed against the wall to prevent it from caving in on top of us. We remained there until the storm ended around 7:30 Monday morning.

When we emerged from the remains of the house, we faced a scene that resembled a war zone. Neighbors' homes that had been multistory were now one story. Bedroom furniture partially hung out of broken windows or missing walls. Every tree was down covering all the roads. Huge cement power poles were snapped in half. The only way out of our destroyed neighborhood was on foot, and even that was dangerous. It was impossible to make a phone call. Even if you had a cell phone it wouldn't work because all of the cell phone towers had been destroyed. Neighbors emerged from their homes in shock, covered with rubble that had fallen on them. Everyone was desperate to let loved ones know that they had survived the storm, but it was impossible to reach them.

The aftermath

We've all seen news reports and pictures of storm victims after a tornado, hurricane, fire, flood, earthquake, tsunami, or mudslide. What we don't often see are images of those same victims six to nine months later when they are still trying to remember what they have lost. They may still be picking through rubble searching for important mementos or photographs that are part of their memories. And if any are found they are often badly damaged and unsalvageable. The victims are still struggling to work with insurance companies and government agencies to get the resources needed to rebuild their lives.

How do I know this? My home was destroyed with all of the contents inside. It took five weeks to get an insurance adjuster to visit my home and nine months to rebuild it. However, this could be considered minor compared to the aftermath for victims of tornadoes, fires, and floods. Following all disasters, rebuilding homes and lives takes an extensive amount of time and effort.

My personal outcome was filled with many life lessons—most of them negative. Like many other victims I suffered with post-traumatic stress. A side effect of that was the inability to make a comprehensive insurance claim because I couldn't remember what I owned before the storm. For many years following the disaster, memories came back reminding me of items that I never claimed, totaling thousands of dollars.

Realizing that I could have prevented many of the negative outcomes, I took on a mission to make sure no one else makes the same mistakes. There is a book in progress with the details, but this plan will help you get started.

1. Even if you don't live in Tornado Alley, along the coast, in an earthquake zone, or in a flood-prone area, don't feel that you will avoid a natural disaster. Storm patterns are changing. And fires are a potential hazard in all areas.

2. Now is the time to take stock of your possessions before a storm is headed your way. Stand in the center of each room in your home/apartment/office and determine what if anything is precious, critical, irreplaceable. Make note of these items so that you can decide how you will protect them as you make preparations. Don't forget overlooked areas like the garage, basement, attic, or detached structures.

3. If you have pets, it is critical that you plan for their safety well in advance. If you have to evacuate to a shelter, your pets may not be able to stay with you. Pets are often more traumatized by major storms than their guardians, so it is extremely important to consider their needs as well as your own.

4. Review your insurance policy to determine what is covered in the case of a natural disaster. Have there been any major changes or acquisitions since the policy was written? Do you need separate coverage for more expensive items or special business equipment? For small businesses, do you have a business continuity policy to cover the financial loss if your business must close because of a storm or disaster? Note that you may need a special policy to cover floods, and those policies must be purchased a minimum number of days before a weather event.

5. Do you know your neighbors? After a major disaster you may depend on your neighbors more than you do now, so be neighborly and introduce yourself. It is a great idea to exchange contact information as well as phone numbers for friends and family members.

6. It is critical to make a photo inventory of your home—every room, closet, cupboard, drawer, and storage space. These pictures do not have to be perfect but they should be clear enough to help you remember all of your possessions after a disaster. At least two copies of this photo inventory should be stored in separate locations. This is critical to help you complete a comprehensive insurance claim and obtain the reimbursement needed to help you rebuild your life.

7. Once you have determined the paperwork and possessions that are most critical, create a grab-and-go file that you could use if you needed to evacuate your home quickly. This file should have a handle and the ability to maintain files for your family, pets, and possessions. For items that cannot fit into this file, have a plan for how you would remove them in an emergency situation.

8. Plastic bins are your friends. As a photographer, I had thousands of printed pictures before Hurricane Andrew threatened. I stored all of these pictures in sealed plastic bins in the bottom of a closet and didn't lose one picture! This is the only thing I did right before the storm. The rest of these suggestions are based on all of the things that I should have done, but didn't.

Disasters bring out the best and the worst of society. Looters found their way to my neighborhood within hours after the end of the storm. Price gouging for batteries, ice, and water was a sad fact of life. There were not enough police or National Guard personnel to protect the massive area of destruction. However, there were many more people who took it upon themselves to serve as traffic officers in intersections with no signals. Others volunteered in the soup tents that were set up in the worst areas. My prayer is that you will realize the hardships felt by individuals and families after a major weather event and offer your emotional or financial support if possible.

The number of natural disasters is increasing. If you are facing one of these unfortunate events, please heed the warnings of your local and national officials. And if you have followed the suggestions in my plan, rest easy knowing that your disaster experience will not be followed by a financial and emotional disaster. I wish you many blessings for a safe and secure future.

Chapter 30

My journey

by Lhea Scotto-Laub

Lyme disease was always something that other people got, and I believed it was rare, so why should I be concerned? After all I am not very outdoorsy, and I don't live in Connecticut or near any woods. I didn't know that is was growing ten-fold in the United States and not just in Connecticut—or on the east coast for that matter. Once I realized that I was getting sicker and a nontraditional doctor told me that he believed that I had third stage Lyme, I realized that I had a difficult road ahead of me. I still assumed that I would just get an antibiotic and be fine. Wow, was I wrong. Without a definitive diagnosis, no traditional doctor would give me antibiotics. Now my journey to get better, had to begin.

Growing up on Long Island, New York, in middle-class America seemed fine to me. I was physically well, lived a healthy lifestyle, and as a child went to the doctor every year for checkups. As a young adult, I became interested in a holistic lifestyle and maintained it throughout my life. I was always a happy, high-energy person, packing a lot of living into each day. In adulthood I was never hospitalized for any medical issues other than the birth of my three sons who are now in their thirties. It wasn't until 2012, at the age of sixty-one, that I started to feel symptoms that something was not right with me.

In the beginning of my non-confirmed Lyme disease, I felt intermittent chills, swollen glands, and a stiff neck. I also had some headaches, which I hardly ever had before. I thought I had picked up a virus from someone, since I have grandchildren and meet people for business purposes. I recalled seeing an internist in 2011 or so. He had asked me if I was a runner because my pulse was low for someone my age; it was around fifty-eight beats per minute. I said that I was active and did some running in my earlier years and blew the whole thing off while thinking that my heart was just really working well.

Prior to feeling ill, I was extremely stressed and believe that my immune system was compromised. The company I owned took a big hit due to the economy in 2008, and I was not able to recover financially. Additionally, my husband and I were downsizing to a smaller house. After the move, which was physically and emotionally traumatic, I got floaters in my eyes.

As the days passed, I found myself growing more and more tired, I was having confusion and memory loss. I blew this off too, since I believed that this was due to the aging process. I ignored other symptoms as well, and as time went on I was not multitasking well, found it harder to make decisions, and viewed things I had handled easily in the past, now as overwhelming. I began to become sensitive to light, and this began to impair my driving at night. After wearing reading glasses for years, I was having trouble seeing street signs at night, and the glare from the street lights and oncoming cars was unbearable to me; it was becoming a safety issue. In 2013 I went to the ophthalmologist to see if I could have cataract surgery and even though I had very minute cataracts I convinced him that they must have been impairing my vision. Well, he corrected both eyes, one month apart. My vision was better but the glare was still there. I had no idea that the glare issue could be coming from the Lyme.

During 2014 I was having night sweats that continued to grow worse. I was postmenopausal and really could not figure this out. I started to have joint pain, specifically my knees and hips, again thinking that it was my age. I had trouble with balance, and standing up from a crouched position was difficult. I had heightened emotional sensitivity and found myself crying often, which was not typical behavior. I also felt burning on the bottom of my feet.

I noticed that I was no longer having a sound night's sleep. I would awaken several times a night due to nightmares, leg cramps, and/or increased urination. This was also not typical of past behavior. Again, I thought it was part of my aging process (duh). As my symptoms progressed, I started to get a stinging sensation in my arms and legs; it was like insects were biting me, but there was nothing there. I began to question my sanity! I was starting to feel extremely fatigued. My heartbeat began to beat faster at times, and I was starting to feel faint. It is important to note that I had never fainted in my entire life.

One day I was having lunch with my lifelong friend when I started to feel strange. I felt like my heart was not beating right; I felt light headed and breathy. I said that maybe I was nervous and thought that if I just had eaten some food I would feel better. Then I had a dentist appointment a day later. I was there for a six-month cleaning. When I got up out of the seat, I was the extremely dizzy and nauseous, and of course I thought that I had eaten something that did not agree with me. It never dawned on me that there was something serious going on inside of me.

There were neurological issues happening to me as well. I was forgetting where I was when I was driving, I was missing exits and taking wrong turns. As a professional writer—forgot to tell you that—I was noticing that I was writing and leaving out letters. When I typed at the computer I was making many more errors than usual. I also noticed that my thought processes were impaired. I have a very good vocabulary and excel at word games, but I was unable to think of words that I use daily to solve word puzzles. Additionally, I was leaving on lights and the stove. I was misplacing things . . . more than before (LOL). I noticed sporadic pains in my chest, which turned out to be from my heart rate dropping, and then my heart pumping quickly to compensate for the drop in blood pressure. If it weren't for this I would have fainted. As my symptoms progressed, my head was beginning to bob up and down a little to the left.

During this time there were doctors' visits and, even though I was seriously deteriorating, there did not appear to be sincere interest in my case since the blood tests were negative for Lyme. Yes, there were many blood tests, but not all blood tests and labs are equal, as I have learned. Yes, I was referred to a cardiologist. But, there were no positive results from anything. My second cardiologist, after a stress test, wanted me to get a pacemaker, saying I had third stage heart block. The third cardiologist put me on a Holter monitor for a whole month and concluded that I did not need a pacemaker; he said that my heart was in the normal range.

I lost my upbeat personality and sense of humor. I was taking naps during the day, yet still feeling exhausted. I was struggling to see clients, and it was becoming more difficult to formulate thoughts in my head or on paper. Many doctors said that I had Lyme symptoms but my tests were negative. They checked for MS and other similar illnesses. They asked me if I had been in the woods lately and if I ever had a bull's-eye rash on my body. Firstly, I was very confused and had memory loss at that time; secondly, I could have had the Lyme in my body for years before it came out. Thirdly, according to specialists in the field, you don't have to have a bull's-eye rash to have contracted Lyme. I was in the woods in Massachusetts for about a week on two separate occasions. That occurred about 2010–2011. Do I remember getting bit? Not really, but mosquitoes have always been attracted to me. I can get 50–100 bites in a summer. So, I am not sure if I had a tick bite. In fact, Dr. Dietrich Klinghardt, MD, PhD, a leading authority on neurologic disorders, mentioned in an article on Dr. Joseph Mercola's website July 29, 2015, that when a tick bites you, it numbs the area and that we do not always see the bite because it could be in our scalp or other not normally checked area of the body. Also, it is important to note that I had my dog with me at the time. Dogs can carry ticks too, as do other animals (also mentioned in the article). I did spray her with a flea and tick spray, but who knows if that worked. There is a chance that she brought the tick home.

Well, if it wasn't for my husband's best friend, Dr. Howard Robins, I may not have found a solution to my serious physical and mental decline. Dr. Robins is a leading authority on intravenous ozone. He observed my neurological and cardiac decline, as well as my overall symptoms and realized that I had a serious problem with the electrical system of my body. He used an unconventional treatment called intravenous ozone therapy, which is unconventional in the United States, but used regularly in Europe. He uses O_3 and injects the gas into your arm. It just takes a few minutes. It is said to kill bacterial infections and viruses. Yes, it worked! It was a long haul. I went for treatments five mornings a week starting May 2014. I recently reduced my treatments to three, days per week and will be done, I hope by the end of 2015. I feel sensational and I finally have my life back!

People ask me how I know that ozone was responsible for my return to health. I can tell you that it worked for me. I was never on any medications or received other assistance in my recovery other than the ozone therapy. Additionally, I have seen it work for other people. One person who is a diabetic was not responding to antibiotics and was going to potentially have her leg amputated. I saw her have ozone treatments and become healed of the ulcers on her legs.

Today I am stronger, both emotionally and physically. I no longer feel my heart racing to compensate for low beats and low blood pressure. I feel clearheaded too. I have so much more energy and when I am driving at night, there is no glare. I truly feel that I have been given a second chance at life.

Possessing a strong sense of humanity, I pass this story along to you so that I may potentially help you, a loved one, or a friend.

Chapter 31

Wisdom for finding your purpose

by Lisa Marie Jenkins

When I was eight years old, my father died abruptly and my mother became emotionally unavailable for many months. I can distinctly remember believing that I was not as good as other people, because I didn't have a dad. The feeling snowballed into a major inferiority complex throughout most of my childhood.

Around adolescence, I began blossoming and observing people in the world that appeared powerful and of high-esteem. I made the decision that the more insecure I felt in any situation, the higher I would hold my head to appear outwardly confident. I began emulating people that I admired. Though this started as a coping mechanism when feeling insecure and intimidated, I unknowingly was learning how to "act as if" and eventually I truly did become confident.

In the business world this attitude, born of my childhood trauma, worked to my advantage, and I confidently pursued my career. It was natural for me to bite off more than I could chew and stay focused on what I brought into a situation or position, and then trusted that I could figure the rest out as I went along. I spent more than twenty years in senior sales and marketing roles at hi-tech Fortune 500 companies and was recognized as one of the 200 most influential women in my industry. I went after what I wanted, stayed focused on my goal, not on what I lacked, and didn't let fear immobilize me; nor did I get caught up in proving myself first or seeking perfection.

In my personal relationships, specifically the romantic ones, I could not have been more opposite. My childhood wounds of feeling abandoned, and subsequently "less than," translated into "I am not okay without a man." Over and over again, I gave my power and worth away to keep a boyfriend, partner, or husband. It was a pattern that created immense suffering throughout much of my adult life and led me on a spiritual journey and down the path of a fifteen-year personal development journey to find peace and happiness within myself.

Then, as if a brick hit me over the head, my purpose came to me with total clarity. It was a knowing from deep within me that emerged, "Oh this is why I am here!"

I learned there were many women in the world experiencing the same thing that I had experienced. I knew with certainty from my healing and transformation on the personal side that I was whole, with or without a man. That sense combined with my years in a successful male-dominated corporate career had groomed me perfectly to work specifically with professional women. An inner knowing from deep within me allowed me to realize that I was meant to work with other women to develop the clarity, courage, and confidence to play big and lead authentically to help transform the world with heart. I could use my experience to encourage other women to use their inherent natural feminine strengths. I love working with women to ignite their own passion and purpose, and most importantly help them realize that they are the one that they have always been waiting for.

I now work as a professional speaker and executive coach to create a bridge that connects the conventional business world to personal development and mindfulness—I have a career I love!

Time and energy wisdom

Spend time with people who energize you and support your dream. The people we spend the most time with become the common denominator for who we are and how we behave and show up in the world. Looking at it in the extreme, if you want to become a highly evolved person who wants to make positive changes in the world, hanging out with drug addicts or gang members will not support you in rising upward. Now I know that sounds really silly. But, if everything is energy, what or whom we hang out with, has a huge effect on vibration—even when those people are only slightly below where we want to be. Whoever is in our proximity the most will be the common denominator for determining at what level we think and behave. The company you keep is critical in determining your success. Try this exercise.

1. Determine the seven people in your life you spend the most time with.

2. Write their names on a list.

3. Place a plus sign next to each person who is a positive and supportive influence in your life. In other words, you feel great around them, you enjoy being with them, they uplift and support you, and they give you energy.

4. Place a minus sign next to the people you spend time with that are difficult and take a lot of effort to be around. In other words, they bring you down; they can suck the life out of you.

If there were no minus signs on your list, you are way above average in ensuring that you surround yourself with supportive people. Congratulations! If you have one or more minus signs next to people in your life, I bet these relationships are ones that feel obligatory. They are probably family members or someone that has been in your life a long time, possibly a spouse or long-time friend.

Here is where you can start becoming conscious and fully aware of who you give yourself and your time to. It is critical for your own journey inward and upward to only give yourself to those that give fully back. If they don't feed you, it's time to take a look at drawing some healthy boundaries in those relationships. Remember, you have to be your biggest supporter and keeper of the gate of your energy. If the ones that bring you down are family members, it may mean you learn to detach and love them from afar. It means that you choose how much time and energy you offer those relationships. If they only take from you and there is no return at all, detach and move on. Those people are like cancer to your spirit and self-worth. Think of a hot air balloon. The only way to rise up in the sky is to start dropping the sand bags. People in your life can be doing the same thing to you, holding you down. They can become weights that keep you from transcending to success, happiness, and your dreams.

Let go of feeling responsible for anyone else's journey in life. You are not God; it's arrogant for us to think we are responsible for another person's life or life experiences. That belief only keeps us from focusing on our own life, which we are totally responsible for. It's not your job to sacrifice yourself or allow yourself to suffer. Not only is this behavior counterproductive for your own life, it doesn't support or help the other person either. The most loving thing you can offer another person is to be a role model for healthy boundaries and taking care of yourself first. Whether or not they choose to shift is not your business. You are your business. You are the one and only thing you can control during your life.

Let's say you are starting a new venture, getting married, getting divorced, or changing careers, and your mother is not supportive and tells you all the reasons you shouldn't do it. You don't have to engage with her or have her approval; you only need your own approval. Her opinion is based on her experience and filters, along with her own fear. It doesn't mean she doesn't want the best for you. My own mother was notorious for telling me how I should decorate or how I should be raising my kids. To me, her unsolicited opinions came across as criticism, and I would immediately become defensive. It created a lot of arguments and conflict in our relationship, and it usually left me feeling like I was never good enough. This one response alone could have drastically changed the dynamics of our relationship: "Thanks for sharing your thoughts or feelings, but this works for me." This one statement alone can save a lot of drama in our lives. It also requires letting go of needing someone's approval, but the gift you receive is the ability to tune into your own innate wisdom, which always knows what is best for the highest good.

part *five*

BARS: service

Chapter 32

Service

by Nancy Fox

"Service is a smile. It is an acknowledging wave, a reaching handshake, a friendly wink, and a warm hug. It's these simple acts that matter most, because the greatest service to a human soul has always been the kindness of recognition."
Richelle E. Goodrich

Service is a selfless act that benefits others. Service is what people do for others without expecting anything in return. Many times the service that people recognize is from volunteers throughout the world who serve in a disaster, meet needs in a community, advocate for a cause, educate the public about a health concern, serve meals to people who are disadvantaged, or raise funds to help an individual, family, or cause. Richelle E. Goodrich suggests something even more simplistic as service, such as acknowledging others and sharing kindness. All of these examples are service, and many women are gems at providing service for others.

Another way to serve is to help in some way with a product or service. Have you thought about creating a product or service that would make lives simpler or create good feelings, or actually starting an organization to support someone or a group facing a challenge? Maybe you already provide one of these services to others. Look back at the many women in history to determine who has provided service to others. In fact, there is very little chance that the women in history, or you, have served others with a product or service without using the elements of service that Goodrich indicated in her quote. Will you serve others with more awareness of your contribution from this moment forward? Will you align your service with your beliefs or will you meander to serve as needed with causes that arise? However you choose to serve, you are touching the lives of those in the present and you may be changing the future for many.

The women mentioned so far in this book and those whose stories are included have served as role models for other women. For instance, Rosa Parks led women and people of color to stand up for equal rights, changing the course of present-day interactions and opportunities. Her initial reasoning was to gain self-dignity and respect, and that led to acknowledging the rippling effects for others like her who were not treated with dignity and respect. Louisa May Alcott shared the contrast of young women's roles and the desires of their hearts to develop their unique gifts in the book *Little Women*. Indira Ghandi created an agricultural program feeding many and creating jobs for women around the world. Monte Skall directs a national nonprofit organization that serves many patients who struggle with a disease laden in controversy by two sides of the medical field by fighting for legislation to promote education and doctor protection.

While serving others as the fundraiser for my sons'

wrestling team, volunteering at my church, participating in organizations, and being involved in many other avenues of service, I was unaware of my impact on the people I was serving. I was simply raking in the joy I received by helping others or focusing on the particular cause at the time. I was (am) a meanderer. Are you confused about how your service to others will benefit them? Are you wrapped up in the joy that you receive in helping others? If you are meandering through your life serving, are you doing so with purpose? I am challenging you to serve with joy and purpose, if you are not already doing so. First of all, I am not discounting the contributions you are giving as you meander through the world of service. The world needs meanderers to assist in time of need. Second, some of us need a meandering cause or service from time to time in our lives. I am posing the challenge that you were designed to be here at this time to create or participate in something that is more than the myriad of service possibilities and to serve in a way you have not imagined. This is service that aligns with your beliefs, benefits yourself, provides actions that will impact a person or group, and brings results that will totally fill you to the brim of passion, compassion, and love for self and others.

Many times people say that serving isn't about you. Sheri Dew, in the book *Saying It Like It Is* wrote, "True leaders understand that leadership is not about them but about those they serve. It is not about exalting themselves but about lifting others up."[1] This is true, and I am proposing service begins with you, your beliefs, and the benefits that you desire so that you can take action that serves others and gain results for all involved. This is best illustrated in the myriad of service opportunities. You may or may not want to travel abroad to serve. You may want to serve children in a girls or boys club or mentoring in an educational setting. Serving relates to your interest and skills. Sometimes service does take us out of our comfort zone and teaches many things we may not have learned had we stayed with what we know and are comfortable doing. Growth and a sense of contribution are essential needs of human beings to connect on a spiritual level with self and others.

Chapter 33

Wake up, choose you, and decide to be happy

by Bonnie G. Hanson

I had one hand on the screen, ready to push the handle and walk out the front door when something made me turn around and look at the scene before leaving the house. Gazing back into what felt like a war zone, I saw my living room filled with well-used furniture, a fussy husband, crabby kids, and a barking dog. It was truly a scene from the "Calgon . . . take me away" TV commercials of the 70s. This was *not* the life I'd imagined for myself. Although I had finally made it to my dream house with the white picket fence, that was the only piece of my world remotely close to resembling a fairy tale. My life looked good on the outside but on the inside it was chaos. I was a mess.

After another frustrating "conversation" with my significant other, all I could hear was the voice of Wayne Dyer in my head saying, "We teach people how to treat us." *What?* How could that be true? I certainly didn't teach anyone to treat me like this. Shaking my head in disbelief at my own thoughts, the rant continued in my head, "I don't get it. I'm a good person. I'm working my tail off! How could I have 'taught' my family to be so miserable? This is not how I pictured things would be. How can this be my life?" I wanted to deny it, but deep down I knew that Wayne's words were true, and that I was the common denominator connecting all of the unhappy dots. The myriad of unhappiness I saw was simply a reflection of my own sadness and depression. I was tired, lonely, and hurt from trying so hard and feeling like I was spinning my wheels getting nowhere. I was a yes-woman, wife, mother, business owner, and volunteer; and I was utterly exhausted. I had no time for myself, and I had no boundaries.

For so long, I felt like my life was just happening to me, one curveball after another. What a miserable way to live—constantly striking out as a victim of circumstance. The definition of insanity is to keep doing the same thing over and over again and expecting a different result. If I wanted things to change, the change must begin with me.

That was the day I woke up to realize that the truth I had recently learned was absolutely true: *I am responsible for my own happiness.* My attitude is my choice, and the lens through which I view the world is completely up to me. Whether I live in a friendly or a hostile universe is my choice. The time had come to draw my line in the proverbial sand. It was time to start saying "no" to some of the demands my life and my family placed upon me and to start saying, "yes" to me and to my well being. This was *my* time!

The first step to making a change begins with a decision. This decision was mine alone: to take control and start creating my life by choice instead of simply allowing life to happen to me by default. Viktor Frankl, epic author, teacher, and holocaust survivor teaches that there is a space between stimulus and response. It is in this space that we find our ultimate power . . . the power to choose our response to any stimulus. Armed with my new plan of taking full responsibility for my life, setting boundaries, and scheduling "me" at the top of the to-do list, I was excited to learn more and experience what freedom from the chaos would feel like. At the same time, it was terrifying to anticipate what the unknown reactions to the "new" me might be.

Like any new choice that turns into a habit, there is a period of transition. First it's shiny and new, then the test of commitment sets in. Will you love yourself enough to continue taking care of you? It took time for both me and my family to adjust. There were absolutely days and weeks that felt like I was riding a rollercoaster, because it's so easy to default back into what's comfortable. Our comfort zone is the menace of mediocrity and, as I've learned, a slow and painful death. We are either growing or decaying, improving or declining as people, achieving or abandoning our dreams, all the while our primitive lizard brains are seeking safety, survival, and the illusion of stability.

As I chose to leave neglect and guilt behind, I began creating new habits and routines to continue to expand my mind and to take proper care of myself. Choosing what defines your personal happiness versus living up to someone else's vision of what defines happiness for you takes immense courage. You do not need permission or acceptance or approval from anyone else in the world in order to be happy. You are free to choose. Do not delay. This is your life!

Often the two worlds collide as what you must do takes priority over what you want to do. Find ways to fill up your "feel-good" tank and layer them with your maintenance activities whenever possible. Walk the dog and listen to a great audio—you are outside, exercising and caring for the dog and yourself all at once. (At the beach is even better!) Countless times I would wind up reading in the bubble bath or listening to an audio or a webinar. That's okay! Find ways to maximize your time and combine your well-being with your must-be-done activities. Begin to practice responding to life and to circumstances instead of simply being reactive. Take time to pause, consider, and reflect and then respond.

During this expanded self-care, I learned a foundational principle that holds true for all of us. Our thoughts are "things." Our thoughts take root in our reality, whether they are negative or positive, so choose wisely. From our thoughts emerge our feelings and emotions, which create the filter that colors our view of the world. Those emotions influence the actions (or inactions) that produce our results. The compounding of our results creates our situations. Remember this theme with the acronym TEARS (Thoughts, Emotions, Actions, Results, Situations) and understand that you can either choose TEARS of joy or TEARS of sorrow. You have the ultimate say, moment by moment, each and every day.

Happiness is a choice and a state of being, not the result of receiving something outside of you or something you feel momentarily because someone was nice or did something for you. Do not make your happiness contingent on the approval or actions of others, but rather let it be the result of your choice and decision to be a happy person and lead a happy life. When I changed the information I allowed into my brain and stopped watching the (bad) news, I created a space for choice, a quiet space where I can listen to my inner voice, my inner truth, and connect with what I really need and desire to fulfill me. This personal attention to your inner voice provides you with the opportunity to build self-trust and rely on your inner voice while merely giving consideration to the outer voices (of family, friends, media) attempting to influence you. Choose to be positive and allow your happiness to be the result of the life you choose to lead.

By placing myself at the top of the to-do list and choosing me, I look and feel better and have more energy from exercising, eating well, and generally taking better care of my brain and my body. The results are better sleep, more patience, and less stress. This creates more resilience when things go sideways, and I am more optimistic in my outlook on life. All in all, my family has adjusted well to my new routines, and they are now empowered to handle situations and tasks on their own, things that I once provided the solutions for. My life isn't perfect, and I still have ups and downs just like you, but it is significantly better than being smacked by curveballs and far better than striking out on a daily basis!

Let's face it; the world is full of strikeouts and imperfection. We all make mistakes. It's part of what makes us human, and the blemishes are what create our individuality and uniqueness. However, all of us have said or done some thing(s) we regret at some point in time (or is it just me?). It can be easy to get caught up in that space of regret, sadness, shame, or guilt that keeps us feeling like we're stuck in quicksand and not able to move forward. In life, if we keep the accent on learning (AOL) instead of leaving situations to chance or luck (SOL), we can always find a positive solution.

The following is a three-step process to shift "epic fail" to a "win":

A—acknowledge and accept. Whatever happened, happened. Often, the meaning we apply to a situation is far worse than the actual event. Accept that this "thing" occurred. Acknowledge and accept it without judgment. It's not right or wrong, it just is.

O—own it. Take responsibility for the situation. What was your role or contribution? How did you act, react, or behave? Even if you "didn't do it" or something was done to you, what was the part you played in the event that's keeping you stuck? Why is it holding you hostage?

L—learn, love, and leave it. What can you learn from this experience? What will help you from this point forward in your life? What's the lesson that this situation has taught you? Can you find the gift? Share the love and extend forgiveness to all involved, including you. Again, no judgment about right or wrong. Forgiveness allows you to release the negative, the anger, or bitterness. It does not condone the situation or act. Decide to move on and leave this lesson behind. Lesson learned. Duty complete. If it comes up again, you will now have a clearer perspective to reframe it and move forward.

Maturity, responsibility, and self-care go hand in hand. Self-care is not selfish. Self-care is loving yourself (the PG version) and creating a solid foundation from which you can be selfless (this is a win). Now you can give from an overflow of energy and desire (win) instead of giving until depleted and resentful. A huge difference! As you practice being the best version of you, you give the people in your life permission to do the same (win). Anytime we can create a win-win-win, the world is definitely a better place because of it.

Try this on and see if it's a fit for you. Practice a positive psychology approach to your life. Use this focus: What's the best-case scenario and what is going right with you? Build on that and follow the framework below to make each day better and better. You have waited long enough. It feels good to feel good and you deserve this!

Positivity. Make the decision to be happy. Choose optimism. Practice resilience. Keep a victory log: at the end of each day record three items that are wins for you. (Do this before bed so you plant the positive in your subconscious.) If feeling low, refer to your log to help build yourself back up. Create a playlist of positive videos or songs. Start your day on the right note. Be grateful to be alive. Keep a gratitude journal. (Keep a gratitude journal about a person in your life. Give it to him or her as a gift.)

Engagement. Identify your strengths and make choices from this space. Focus on the things you are great at and love to do, and hire or delegate your weaknesses. Your weaknesses are someone else's strengths, and they *love* doing these things. You will make them happy and create great teamwork. Find what lights you up and do more of that. The world needs more people feeling alive and energized.

Relationships. Be you. Be authentic. Be honest. Build high quality connections with others by being truly interested in them and asking great questions that allow them to reveal who they truly are. Seek first to understand, then to be understood. Be kind (especially to yourself). If you wouldn't say it to a friend, don't do it or say it to yourself.

Forgive. Holding bitterness or resentment is like poisoning your own mind and body. Forgive yourself and forgive others. Surround yourself with amazing people.

Meaning. Practice being in awe of life. Enjoy the fascinations of nature, people, and the planet. Pursue your purpose for being here or uncover your life purpose by moving in the direction of your dreams or the things that bring you joy. Follow your passions. Find what motivates and fuels you. What is really important to you? Use this intrinsic motivation with grit and determination to help you move toward your mission. Cultivate an attitude of contribution. Contribute time, energy, or money to causes you are passionate about. Relish in your spirituality. Play! The meaning of life is to enjoy it.

Achievement. Control your focus. Discipline your digital distractions. Begin with the end in mind. Be intentional. Determine where you want to go and work backwards to set up the timeline. Set goals using positive language and deadlines. Chunk down the goal into smaller pieces. Schedule each phase or task. Work in blocked time on a single task or project until complete. Maybe you only have thirty minutes a day, but be consistent. Consistency is the key. The compounding of daily, consistent action creates big results. Focus on the step you're working on, and then focus on the next step. Small is huge. Enjoy the process. Don't worry about the big prize. Follow the plan and don't confuse busy with productive. Look at your outcomes. Results never lie. Celebrate your wins!

Vitality. Whatever your size, shape, or situation, love your body. There is a connection between your mind and body—keep it positively charged. Your physical state will determine your mental state. If you need a boost . . . move! Food is fuel; use it that way. Be aware of your emotions. Are you looking for love in a chocolate chip cookie? Stop it! Create that satisfaction elsewhere (by adding more meaning and awesome associations). Put more joy into your life. For body and mind both: garbage in, garbage out. Be active. Some people avoid exercise but keep in shape having fun. Have more fun! Drink water. Breathe. Really! Practice breathing every day: Breathe in to a count of seven; hold for twenty-one counts; exhale in fourteen counts. I do ten reps every day. Moving your body generally promotes better sleep, which can lead to clearer thinking, more patience, and less stress. Life is for living, not stressing. Find what makes you feel alive and do more of that. Live out loud. The world needs more of YOU!

As actress and drama teacher Uta Hagen said, "Overcome the notion that you must be regular. It robs you of the chance to be extraordinary."

Chapter 34

The day I almost lost my life

by Katie Humphrey

Making good decisions isn't something I was always good at doing. In my late teenage years and early twenties, my choices mainly consisted of partying, spreading negativity, and spending more than I earned. I frequently drank too much alcohol and smoked cigarettes, thinking I was indestructible. Everything that came out of my mouth was either a complaint or gossip. My thoughts were full of body bashing and criticisms of others and myself. I was miserable. To make myself feel better, I used the majority of my paychecks to fund my substance abuse and party lifestyle.

I often felt life nudging me to make a change. I wondered if there could be a more purposeful life available for me. And deep down, I wanted to be someone that mattered, to do something that left the world in a better place. Though, as much as life sent me these gentle nudges, I ignored any such notion. I chose to continue on a self-destructive path until the day it almost cost me my life.

After enduring a triad of devastating blows, including a horrendous breakup, being diagnosed with a health condition known as polycystic ovarian syndrome (PCOS), and gaining thirty pounds in less than three months, I hit rock bottom. The face of each new day brought more pain as I grieved over my broken heart. Meanwhile, I felt like a young woman going through menopause with the symptoms from my condition, and my bloated body only reminded me of how toxic I felt. It was almost too much to bear.

To deal with it all, I drank. And the more I consumed alcohol, the more disgusted I was with myself. I didn't want to live this way anymore. My life had become something of a nightmare, and I was the only one to blame.

I desperately wanted to change, so I decided to quit drinking and give up my poor choices. While this seemed like a good decision, my lifestyle changes were only temporary. I was trying to give up my habits without making a real internal shift. The next time I faced a hardship, I went back to my old ways. It was a rough week at work, and I decided to go out with a group of friends to our usual watering hole. Wallowing in my frustration, I had a few too many drinks.

Instead of staying at a friend's house that lived within walking distance of the bar, I chose to drive home. This one decision changed everything. The only thing I remember is waking up to a police officer attempting to put my car into park. I had fallen asleep at the wheel and miraculously kept my foot on the brake through seven light changes. I was pulled from the car and carried to safety.

That night, the eve of Easter, I slept on a concrete floor in jail. My stomach was sick and my head was swimming with thoughts of my life. I considered every decision I had made up until that point and whether or not I was truly living the life I wanted—the life for which I was born to fulfill. I also realized that in one moment, it could have all been over. I could have killed myself or another person, the latter being something I could never fathom having to live through.

I knew it was time for me to make a new life. From that moment on, I had to change from the inside out. I started with my mindset, including the very thoughts and beliefs I held. This affected the words I spoke and rippled over to my every action. I decided to behave as if I was already living my desired life. Ideally, this consisted of a positive attitude, a fulfilling career, financial abundance, and healthy relationships. I began to surround myself with books and information, any kind of knowledge that enhanced my mind and filled me with encouragement. I chose to speak words of love and gratitude and made decisions every day that brought me closer to my goals.

Within a year's time, I lost the extra thirty pounds around my midsection, and I completely shifted my PCOS symptoms to a point where I was clear of any trace of the condition. I married my best friend, and we recently celebrated our five-year anniversary by traveling to London, Paris, and Edinburgh, Scotland. I started a business to support women around the world to create healthy, happy, and fulfilling lives. And most importantly, I found my worth and myself. I discovered that just like everyone else, I was made for a unique purpose and meant for so much more than I was experiencing.

I have had the opportunity to travel to exotic locations, live in a beautiful home, and spend time with people who love me. My business exploded into multiple six figures of growth, and most recently, my third book *Elizabeth Hazel and the Day of Desires* was published to share my message and movement with teenage girls. I get to professionally speak, write, and coach on topics that make a difference in people's lives, and every day enhances the amazing adventure I am on. I feel lucky to be alive and make the most of this one life I get to have.

Working with hundreds of different women has allowed me to see what kind of decisions we are all making. Many times, my clients are choosing thoughts, words, and behaviors that don't serve them. Like me in my former life, these women feel oppressed by actions that bring more negativity and frustration into their lives. Once they see that having a different, more desirable life comes by changing from the inside out, they are empowered. This internal shift means forming new thoughts and a mind that supports your dreams. It may not feel easy, but with practice, it becomes a habit that will change your entire life.

Start off each morning by prepping your mind for success. Read books, watch movies, and listen to podcasts that fill you with positivity and uplift your spirit. Spend time with people who support your dreams and encourage you. Give others the sincere compliments, loving energy, and kind words that you want to receive. Be someone who sets the example for other women to follow. Step up and make decisions that others won't. Be in integrity with your desires and make sure you are always working towards your goals. End each day with a gratitude journal, focusing on what is working in your life and finding the blessing in the obstacles. Your perspective will determine the quality of your life, so intentionally direct it in a way that will serve you.

I look back on my experience and feel blessed. My life was spared, and I was given a second chance. Through the entire experience I can see how capable we are as women to take a stand for the life we want right at this very moment. We don't need to hit rock bottom to go after our dreams. It's a vicious lie that it's ever too late to change, or that you're not meant for something greater. Consider all of the challenging times in your life and realize they are opportunities in disguise to choose something better. We don't often see hardships that way, but by shifting your perspective, you will discover how everything you want is possible and waiting for you. And it all starts with one decision.

Chapter 35

Things you'll learn, places you'll go

by Leslie Petruk

My son entered the world on August 2, 2001, after a normal pregnancy and uncomplicated delivery. The journey we were about to embark on would change my life forever. When Brandon was around six months, the pediatrician noticed that he was not meeting his normal developmental milestones and suggested we have some testing done. Approximately three months later we were told that he had a genetic disorder called XYY. The geneticist informed us that "out of any genetic disorders this is probably the best one to have." We were told he may have speech delays and learning disabilities, but there was little research or information on the disorder, so we weren't sure what to expect. We started early intervention, and Brandon received numerous therapies each week to build his muscle tone and help him develop as normal as possible. My life was filled with doctors and therapy appointments, sometimes as many as ten to twelve per week. In addition, our family moved from Austin, Texas, to Charlotte, North Carolina, when I was six months pregnant with Brandon, so I had no support system and was still learning my away around the city.

As Brandon continued to grow, it was apparent that he was significantly delayed, and his language was not developing. I fell into a deep depression and was sure that God had made his first mistake ever by giving me a child with special needs—I didn't believe I could handle it. I was overwhelmed and scared for my child's future.

At Christmas of 2002, Brandon was almost sixteen months old, and our pediatrician ordered an MRI because he still wasn't developing as he should. The initial report came back saying everything was normal. On the day before leaving to travel to Canada to visit my husband's family, we received a phone call from my pediatrician. I could tell from her voice that something was wrong. I called her back and she informed me that the full radiology report had come back stating that Brandon's brain was demyelinating and that he likely had a fatal condition in which he wouldn't live past the age of five. This was a pivotal and life-changing moment, one that I will never forget. It was in that moment that I fell to my knees and told God that I was this child's mother, and that if he wouldn't take him from me, I would do *everything* within my power to raise him to be happy and meet his full potential. I couldn't imagine my life without this sweet child. Approximately seven days later, while still in Canada, we received a phone call that Brandon's scan had been misread. His brain was *not* demyelinating, and he didn't have a fatal condition. This was another pivotal and life-changing moment, and I vowed to keep my promise to do everything I possibly could for this child.

That experience and the decision I made in that moment

has lead me to live and view life so differently. My priorities changed drastically and the little irritations and frustrations in life no longer hold the weight they used to for me. I also kept getting the message through various sources (who didn't know each other) that Brandon had been entrusted to my husband and me to love and care for. By the third time someone spoke those identical words to me, I knew the message was being sent and that I needed to hear it and take it seriously.

I was confident that Brandon was here for a reason, and he was going to have an impact on the world. When he was three years old, the school system pulled his services and refused to provide what they were legally obligated to do. After a grueling trial and three years of appeals, we won the case, and changes were made within the system because of Brandon. In the summer of 2011, after many years of assisting in the advocacy, public education, lobbying, and speaking to the North Carolina legislators, a law dubbed "Brandon's Law" went into effect that allows for a six thousand dollar tax credit for the parents of special needs children in North Carolina. It can be applied towards school choice, doctors and therapy bills, and all of the additional expenses families incur.

I pursued my dream of opening a multidisciplinary counseling center in 2003, and through that I have been honored to work with and support other families going through the challenges of raising children with special needs or chronic illness. I know how lonely and scary that walk can be and the dramatic impact it has on the entire family. I have since downsized my practice in order to be more available to my family—another awakening in regards to my priorities. I can grow my business anytime, but I only have one chance to spend the years with my children before they go off to college.

Brandon is now fourteen years old. He is still nonverbal, uses a communication device to speak, and is in a special education class at school. We still have days that are challenging. I will admit, there are days and times that I have my pity party and envy families who can just pick up and go on a trip or take their family out on a bike ride or for a hike. We are limited on what we can do with Brandon, and vacations are challenging. When he is out of his routine and normal environment, he can become aggressive and hit us. His sisters have had to endure a lot, and there are days that I feel so much guilt and sorrow for them that I can get myself into a serious funk. But then something happens, and I am reassured that it is because of this child that I have been offered so many blessings and met so many wonderful people along the way. A few summers ago as I was helping my youngest daughter pack for a family camp that is for families who have children with special needs, she asked me, "Mom, did you know when Brandon was in your tummy that he was special needs?" To which I replied, "No, sweetie, I didn't." She then asked, "Did God know?" I replied, "Yes, sweetie, he did. Why do you ask?" She then said, "Because when I'm a mommy and I have a baby in my tummy, I'm going to tell God I want a special needs baby because I know how to love them." Priceless.

The commitment I made to make my son's life the best I could wasn't just for him. It was for my two daughters, my husband, and me. I haven't always been perfect at it, but I know what's important and can experience joy unlike I ever could before because of the depth of the sorrow I have felt. My life has been enriched and blessed because of that decision, and having had this experience continues to be a guiding force in every area of my life. When I have choices to make that are important, from this experience I have learned to decide based on whether the decision I make is life-giving or not. If it energizes and excites me and gives me life energy, I know what decision to make. Our lives are not a dress rehearsal, and I have the choice as to how and with whom I spend and give my time and energy—I want to make sure it counts!

Writing became a solace for me when Brandon was young, and one evening when I was focusing on the gratitude of the impact of this one sweet boy I wrote:

> **OH! The Things You'll Learn . . . and the Places You'll Go**
>
> When I think about all of the things I have learned since my son entered the world, it astounds me. Prior to having him, I thought occupational therapy was something people did when they needed help learning skills that would assist them in their jobs. I thought children with special needs were a rare occurrence, and I thought I knew what I was getting into when I decided to have a second child. I know now, that I knew nothing! And now, I know a little more then nothing. The more I learn, the more I realize I don't know—the complexity of the human body and genetics is just so far behind my comprehension. I do know, that the little I have learned makes me want to learn more. When I think about what my life may have been like had my son been "typical" (whatever that means!) and all that I would

have missed out on—it becomes so clear to me what a gift he is.

Because of him, I now know . . .

A lot more about human compassion, the complexity of love, and the power of connection with other parents in my shoes. The depth of sorrow that I thought would consume me, when we were told that he may have a fatal condition, and the joy unlike any other when we found out he did not. To rejoice in the small milestones and accomplishments I used to take for granted. For some of the finest people that our paths crossed and would not trade their friendship for the world, I am thankful. I have more compassion, understanding, and love in my heart and more to share. Not to sweat the small stuff and relish in what a gift each and every day is. I see God's grace more prolifically, and the path I am being lead down as being more meaningful. That I have been blessed with a gift that is greater then even I can comprehend. How to live each day more fully, laugh more, and love even more. The great sorrows I feel when I see other children with disabilities and the admiration for their parents who I know are strong and courageous human beings who were chosen to care for their gift. I see my future more clearly and his less clearly . . . and that's okay. I am supposed to help others who have children with special needs. My time here on earth is much more meaningful and my belief in the power of prayer is so much greater. There are people in the world who are angels on earth. There is a need for more knowledge, education, and support for children and families with chromosome variations. I have great admiration for parents and their children who have walked this road before me and for those who will follow. I will travel to places and meet people who will touch our lives deeply. My son has and will touch more lives because of who he is and the spirit he exemplifies. Because of him I see the power and love of God more clearly. Because of him I have learned that miracles do really happen. Because of him, I now know my life has been forever changed . . . and I am eternally thankful that I, of all people, have been entrusted with this little angel.

Chapter 36

Decisive detective

by Tammy Studebaker

Decisive: settling an issue, producing a definite result, resolute, firm, strong-minded, strong-willed, determined.

I consider myself a strong, decisive woman. If you ask my children and husband, each would say: son—legit; daughter—determined and hard-headed; husband—determined.

Growing up in upstate New York, I knew what I wanted to do when I was sixteen.

I would go to college for business and work in retail management. I would work my way up until I was comfortable enough to not worry about money and would some day have a family and figure out a way to stay home for my kids.

I wanted things I did not have growing up: a stable family (my parents' marriage was over by the time I was eleven years old), a family that had dinner together, a mom that could be home for her kids. I would be the traditional happy soccer mom.

As we are all too aware, life rarely works out as we planned.

I did go to college for my bachelor of science. I got a

good job in an executive training program when I graduated and worked my way up in the retail profession.

I married when I was thirty-two and started a family at the age of thirty-five; my husband was forty, and he had his own successful construction company.

When we had our first healthy child, Parker, I was able to be home with him almost every day.

I had proved myself invaluable for the company I was working with at the time. With my help they created a recruiting and training position that would require me to leave the house only one day a week, and I was given a company car and health insurance.

Life was going pretty well, seems as if my decisiveness had produced great results. I was really living the life I had planned. When my son turned four years old, I had my daughter, Emily.

This is where my plan seemed to fall apart.

Food allergies on steroids

Looking back I can see that Emily's problems started from the moment she was born. I was still recuperating from the delivery when the nurse came in to take a Band-Aid® off her; it left a noticeable mark on her arm. The nurse had never seen an infant with such sensitive skin, but for the time being, the alarm ended there. The lull did not last long. By the time Emily was six weeks old, she had dots all over her face. It looked as if someone had taken a red marker and went to work. I assumed it was baby acne, with no clue of the truth—she had severe food allergies, eczema, *and* asthma. Not knowing any of this, we all expected the marks to clear up. Instead, they continued to spread and then they crusted over, a truly awful sight on an otherwise beautiful baby. This is when the seeds of concern were first planted in me. Our pediatrician suggested it might be from food allergies. *Allergies*, I thought, *how bad can that be*?

I quickly educated myself by looking up information online, speaking with my doctor and others, and seeking out books on the subject. A food allergy is a response from the immune system to a substance; it creates antibodies to attack some substance in the food you ate, which your immune system, either correctly or incorrectly, identifies as harmful or dangerous. It is not the substance that makes you suffer, but the reaction from your body that releases a huge store of chemicals. These chemical substances, called histamines, produce unpleasant little symptoms such as hives, swelling or rash, swelling or itching of the lips, tongue or mouth, a tightness in the chest or horse voice or coughing, stomach cramps, vomiting, diarrhea or nausea, fainting or irregular heartbeat, coughing, wheezing and difficulty breathing, chills, panic, sudden weakness, and even death. The goal is not to make you miserable (although it may certainly seem that way) but to blitzkrieg the offending proteins in the food because your immune system believes they're out to get you. Allergy symptoms can range from a mild case of hives to a potentially life-threatening system shutdown.

Emily was in a state of constant reactivity to my breast milk. It couldn't have been because of "the usual suspects" since they had already been removed. I could only assume her reaction was being caused by something else I was eating.

The rash spread to her head and was turning to scabs. In the dysfunctional ways that babies move, she tried to scratch herself all the time, but didn't know how to coordinate her little fingers. And so scratching didn't work and she cried and cried, making it impossible for anyone in the family to sleep for any length of time. As if that weren't bad enough, Emily's stools were explosive and laced with blood. Back to the pediatrician, who recommended that we try allergy testing. Unfortunately, he said that for a three month old, the tests might not reveal much. Her young body had not been exposed to these foods enough to show reactions in the tests. Her body had not yet built up the fighting IGE genes.

This is how I was living: my family was sleep deprived, my son had just started school and was constantly anxious, and my husband was trying to build a new family home even though he had severe arthritis. I couldn't take care of anyone, because having a newborn sick baby was an all-consuming job. If I wanted my little family to get back on track, the key was a happy baby. I was more exhausted then I realized; my whole family, in fact, was running out of patience. The walls of a house were no matches for a baby's scream. We would snap at each other in ways we never had before. In addition to sleep deprivation (I was actually beginning to starve—literally), I had had to cut so many foods out of my diet to keep my breast milk pure that I could not eat enough to keep myself healthy or maintain my weight.

Tests revealed that Emily's allergies were off the charts. (Dr. Wood, who had dealt with thousands of patients with severe, life threatening allergies, had only seen a handful as sensitive as my daughter.) It had been difficult to give up all of the top eight allergens, which included soy, dairy, wheat, peanuts, tree nuts, fish, shellfish, and eggs, but now that I knew her allergies were off the charts, it was crystal clear that it had been necessary. I may have put my own health in jeopardy, but at least I knew it had been absolutely necessary.

Before the allergy tests had begun, I couldn't have guessed that the number of foods to be eliminated would constitute half the aisles of grocery store.

Everyone in my life, thus far, had seen my weight drop in a gradual way and had seen my appearance change gradually, which I think lead them to a certain kind of absent-minded acceptance. I found, when my mother had come to visit me after several months of not seeing me, that this was a false acceptance. At her first glimpse of me, I watched the expression on her face and then watched her burst into tears. This was the first time she had seen me in months, and she was entirely unprepared for the change. Something was terribly wrong with a person who looked this emaciated. Her youngest daughter now looked like a Holocaust survivor. Even though I had kept her informed, no words can prepare you when an adult child is now skin and bones. I already knew that some of my friends actually believed I was terminally ill—they had no idea that an infant's allergies could have such a drastic effect on the mother.

We tried every formula on the market the nutritionists threw our way that had worked for so many other kids, but not mine. And so the question continued to plague me: how could my daughter be this allergic? What do you do when you're out of options? Our only hope, now, was a nutritionist at Hopkins. Emily needed her own special formula and we set out to find one that she could tolerate.

A real and viable solution finally arrived—a combination

of oils, olive and grape seed—that made a perfect and complete formula. Emily was thirteen months old, and while she still needed suppositories to have a bowel movement, she had finally secured a ticket out of the hell realm. And I was saved, too. Now I could eat like a normal adult while my baby could eat something on a steady basis that didn't make her miserable. Very slowly, with constant input from her allergist, we tried new foods since no one thought she should eat this muck for the rest of her life.

I naturally believed that once Emily stopped scratching and screaming and contorting, once her own body wasn't the enemy, once she got a chance to be a normal baby, our little family would be happy again. But I had underestimated the emotional toll this experience had exacted on every one of us. We were always on edge with the fear that our baby girl would be hit by yet another emergency. Her tiny body was full of unknown dangers, which kept us all on pins and needles. Whenever one child in a family has a demanding problem, all attention is focused on that child and the others are expected to fend for themselves until the crisis is over. There are several attending problems with this scenario: one, the other children still need their mother, and two, you don't really know when a crisis is over, and so you can't let your guard down.

At that point it was not an overstatement to say that we were all suffering from PTSD (Post Traumatic Stress Disorder). My five-year-old had the nervous system of a soldier coming out of a war zone. My husband was worn down mentally and physically—literally all the joints, ligaments, and muscles in his body ached. I (mother and protector) was weak of body and emotionally spent. I had watched my helpless infant go through an amount of pain that would make a lifer at San Quentin break down and weep, and somehow I could not relax into the belief that her suffering was now truly over. Every cry and whimper from her cradle set off an anxiety attack that some new plight was beginning. We were just normal people beset by extraordinary problems without a manual on how to get through the crisis. However, in my mind I believed the crisis was over, and we could now go back to living the life I had decided we were going to live.

Emily was taking dance and piano, and my son was busy with martial arts and soccer, and was in the middle school band playing trumpet. Once again I was sure this was the life we were destined to have. Wow, I was officially a soccer mom!

At the age of eight, Emily's health took a bad turn. We rushed to the hospital when she became ill; she had been throwing up and was suddenly unable to speak and was acting as if she were drunk—it was terrifying. I prayed the entire trip to the ER that we would save her and see her smiling face again. By the time we arrived at the door of the hospital she had to be carried in; she was limp. Her blood sugar had dropped to a 23, and she had pneumonia. I had taken her to the doctor only ten hours earlier and had her examined head to toe. After a week's stay, we were told she had ketotic hypoglycemia along with pneumonia. (Ketotic hypoglycemia is a rare, but serious form of low blood sugar in children.) She had been having dizzy spells and migraines for a few years now, and I had been to several specialists to try to understand what the cause was, with no real answers.

It seemed as if conventional medicine had once again stepped in and helped us. We were able to manage Emily's health with asthma medication and frequent meals.

A family in crisis

As the years went by my husband seemed to be aging rapidly before my eyes. His pain throughout his body was unbearable at times, and he began to get sick at the "drop of a hat." One winter, as both he and my daughter were sucking on a nebulizer to get some relief, I realized my husband needed a doctor to look more closely at what was going on in his body. He had already had a test for Lyme disease on three other occasions, and they had all come back negative, but we went ahead and did another test along with extensive blood work. Once the results of his tests came back, we received a call that no one wants to hear—we were being referred to an oncologist. His white blood cell count and platelets were not those of a healthy fifty year old.

After much more testing was done, we were told that my husband has CLL (chronic lymphocytic leukemia), a blood and bone marrow disease that gets worse slowly and has no cure. This is a disease of a seventy-year-old man; how and why did my husband contract this cancer? As a wife and mother, this news was devastating, although many people said we were "lucky" the CLL was not active and we could still have many happy years together. I was deeply concerned. I knew there was some underlying reason my husband's health was suffering, but we were yet to find the answers.

Two years after my husband's diagnosis, my son was now eleven years old and enjoying life in middle school. We were on a family trip to upstate New York, and on the way there my son began to feel ill. By the time we arrived he had a fever, which began to progress to pain throughout his body. After the first night he continued to feel worse and his fever climbed to 103-104 degrees. I brought him to a health clinic and they did several tests. They also told me that he may have Lyme disease and when we arrived back home we should take him to his doctor and get him tested. I did, and they told me the test was negative, no Lyme disease, this was just a bad summer flu.

From this day on my son's health was never the same. He was very active, he had taken martial arts since he was four years old, and had competed at a national level. He also played soccer and had just completed a three-day, sixty-mile bike tour with some other schoolmates. He was very bright and was taking high school math; his name regularly appeared on the honor roll list. This was all history, now he was sick often and even seemed to develop asthma. He needed to run to the sidelines to suck on an inhaler to get through his soccer games and practice. Then he began to lose weight. He lost ten pounds in a short period of time; my son had acid burning throughout his body so badly that his eyes burned.

I began the journey of going from specialist to specialist to find an answer. One was a GI doctor; I knew we needed to figure out what was happening in his gut. I also suspected celiac disease. Six months earlier I had taken gluten out of my husband's diet to help with inflammation in his body, and now he was unable to eat gluten without getting sick. I had suspected Celiac disease for my husband and knew it was genetic. My son was diagnosed with celiac after the endoscopy, and I thought we had an end to my son's health crisis.

Although we were now living gluten free in our home, my son's health was spiraling out of control. He had brain fog, he could not remember if he took a shower ten minutes after he had stepped out of the shower, and he could not read or divide. His neuropathy was so bad his fingers were turning black at times; many days he could not even walk. He was petrified to sleep and began waking up in the middle of the night unable to breathe. I was relentless with specialists and online looking for answers. I would be up all night worried and praying for an answer out of this hell.

Eight specialists later with no real answers, a leading hospital wanted to admit him and run extensive tests and put him on steroids to help with his inflammation. Something deep in my mind told me this was not the answer I was looking for; however, I had no other options.

This was where I had to step out of my box and look at my son's condition and our path.

Lyme disease

On two previous occasions, Lyme disease has been brought to my attention as a possible reason for my son's ill health. I was a rule follower and believed in conventional medicine. If the specialists were telling me Lyme and other tick borne diseases were not the cause, I should believe them.

I had watched another girl, my son's age, with many of his symptoms pass away the year after she was placed in a medical facility to search for answers. Cause of death was undetermined. I was petrified and was headed to our grocery store to load up on foods for my husband and daughter. I was going to stay with my son at the hospital while they searched for answers.

As I drove to the store that Sunday I prayed, yelled, and screamed in my car for another option. When I arrived at the store a woman, who was a friend and member of my church, was standing outside the store. She saw I had been crying and asked if I was okay. I unloaded on her. She took my hand and told me my son had Lyme disease, and, if I put him in that facility, he would most likely not come out alive, and I needed to seek an LLMD (Lyme literate doctor). Lyme disease is caused by the bacterium Borrelia burgdorferi and sets off an inflammatory reaction in one's body. If not treated within weeks of infection, it can become a chronic, even life-threatening condition.

This was way outside of my comfort zone as a rule follower; however, I asked for an answer and had better listen to the response. Not only was I about to buck conventional medicine, but many other areas in my life would suffer as well. Lyme disease is not an illness that is very well understood, and many people will live their lives with other diagnoses and never know that Lyme was the contributing factor to their loss of any quality of life.

A new path

Once I took the path of a TBD (tick borne disease), my family's life changed in ways I was not fully prepared for. When you buck conventional medicine, people tend to disbelieve your diagnosis. My husband was also diagnosed with Lyme disease along with coinfections that often come along with Lyme. My close friends and even some family members offered no help. They thought I was crazy and did not fully understand how ill my son was. When someone has cancer or another recognized illness with a firm diagnosis and protocol in place, people flock to help. My husband's health had also declined to the point I was dressing and feeding him. We had a nurse coming to our house weekly with bandage changes and IV meds.

I never felt so alone in my life. There were many nights I wondered why my family was given life on this planet. To suffer alone? My sister told me that she felt I was losing my mind and may need to be institutionalized. That caught my attention and made me realize I needed to snap out of my problems and focus on getting my son and husband well.

That night I came close to losing my mind. I got on my knees in my kitchen. I prayed and screamed. I was never highly religious, yet I believed in God. I likened myself to Jesus Christ on the cross and wondered why "God had forsaken me." I sobbed for about thirty minutes. The kids were asleep, but my husband heard me. He picked up the phone and called his sister in Colorado. He said we needed help. She came out a few days later and stayed for a week, then later returned and stayed for another two weeks. On her first day in our house I heard her sobbing in our guest room. I asked what was wrong and she said she had no idea how bad things were. Both my husband and son were in bed most of their days with exhaustion, seizures, and many other health issues.

A new friend also came into my life. She had firsthand experience with her college friend who had been in a bed for three years with TBD. She knew what we suffered was real and tragic. Beth was a true blessing and gift. She called my brother, who wanted to help but did not know how, and asked if he could help with a cleaning lady every few weeks. My church started bringing us meals.

I was always very self-sufficient, so to accept this help, allowing others to step into our lives, especially those I was not close to, was a huge step for me. Yet those that had been the closest were gone, had disappeared; they had their lives to deal with.

My son is seventeen years old today, and although he may never return to his previous health, he is looking at colleges and hopes to become an infectious disease doctor. I often remind my family and myself that throughout this journey we have gained so very much.

My husband started working recently after spending three and one-half years in a hospital bed the majority of the days.

When you have that "turn in the road," most of us take the path of least resistance. It is not easy to step out onto that other road. It's a difficult drive with few others on board with you. The outcome can be wonderful though.

Some family and many of my close friends may never be prepared or challenged to accept that other path, or their time of decisiveness may be very different from mine. They may be fighting something that is not so controversial yet demands a high level of focus and determination.

Just the other day my son told me that he knew his illness would forever change his path of what "might have been," but it was for the better, and he will have a much more focused, fulfilling life.

Although I have fewer friends and a very different life then I was determined to have, I have grown emotionally in so many ways. We did not let this experience define us, yet we allowed it to shape us into a decisive, strong-willed family.

I am most definitely a decisive woman, and I hope I have helped raise two decisive children, who will take the path that will lead them where they want to go, even if it seems impossible.

Chapter 37

Laugh and love your way to health

by Irene Tymczyszyn

The meeting has been set for months. The boardroom is packed with all the high-level executives and key associates. The presentation is ready to go. And I am sweating through my shirt. Not the little sweat circles under the arms. I'm talking fully soaked like I just entered a wet T-shirt contest, and yes of course I am wearing a white suit. Nerves? You would think so, but I love sales, I love people, and I love talking about things I am passionate about. My boss looks at me and is concerned. What's going on?

It was Sunday evening . . . the alarm was set for 6:00 a.m. as usual. Fast forward ten hours, eleven hours, twelve hours . . . ring, ring, ring. I slept through my alarm clock, was so very late for work, missed an important meeting, and felt exhausted all day.

I had gone on a dream trip to Ireland for a week, had a great time despite fighting my lack of energy, and came back to the states at midnight. I opened the door to my condo and stepped into a puddle of water that engulfed my new flip-flops and ran over my toes. I turned on the light—the ceiling was caved in and water and debris were everywhere.

The next week I was pouring creamer into my coffee. I saw the swirl of the creamer hit the coffee in the cup, and that's the last thing I remember when I awoke lying on the kitchen floor with a spoon barely in my hand.

Then I got a call from my dear friend Kate whom I have known since kindergarten. She is more like a sister than just a friend. She was crying, barely able to speak, and told me they just found out her four-year-old daughter has leukemia. What's going on?

I called my dad the next day to tell him about the flood in the condo and to catch up with him. I asked about him first, and he told me he just got back from a doctor's appointment and has skin cancer.

The phone rang and it was my mortgage company. They had a break in and robbery. Some files were stolen, one of which had all my important financial information, and the bank was calling to let me know I was at high risk for identity theft. They wanted to schedule an appointment with me to go through the process of what happens next.

Later that week my boss called me into his office and asked "Irene, what's going on?" I couldn't give him a short answer. I told him about everything that was happening, and he just gave me a hug and said that there are resources that the company has to help during times of high stress. I made an appointment with our human resources director, and she gave me some options, one of which was to take a break, take some time off, and deal with all the personal stuff. She said when that was sorted out and I was ready to come back, my job would still be here. I was shocked at first. I could handle this. I handled a lot worse at different points in my life, and I could get through this. The HR director told me to take the weekend to think about what I wanted to do.

I relaxed the entire weekend, and had a doctor's appointment on Monday morning. At the appointment I told my doctor what was going on. She did a variety of blood tests and told me it was going to take a couple days to get the results. On my way to work after the doctor appointment, I got into an accident, and that's when I knew. I had to do something different. I had to take some time to concentrate on myself, my health, and my life. In that minute when I realized what just happened, I looked at my steering wheel and said a prayer to God, "God, what's going on?" And I got an answer, "Be still, let go, let God!" Just like my very good friend Kathy always has said to me over the past several years.

Be still . . . I have never been one to be still. I was always on the move since I was a little girl. In high school I played sports, had two or three jobs, and was active in several clubs. In college I took extra classes throughout the semester, worked several jobs, and did a variety of internships. Throughout my professional life I was always doing my regular job and prepping myself for the next promotion, the next opportunity, the next city or country where I wanted to move. Be still . . . no way.

As hard as it was, I went to my boss and told him I decided to take some time off. It was so very hard for me because I loved my work, and I have always worked. "Be still, let go, let God" rang in my head.

Nothing could have prepared me for what happened over the next several months, but I now know to trust that little voice in your head—always. I went back to the doctor and thought nothing of it. I thought the blood work would come back and show I needed more iron or something. My doctor said all the blood work came back fine and there was nothing else she could do to help me except to refer me to a psychologist. What? I didn't need a psychologist—I had physical symptoms. I was sweating profusely, I was passing out, and I was exhausted most of the time. I left the office and knew I needed a second opinion. I went to another doctor, and the same thing. A third, and again they found nothing. At this point I thought, okay, maybe I do need a psychologist, so I made the appointment. It was a thirty-minute consult, and in that short time, the doctor said he had a couple of ideas of what was going on with me but he needed to see me again. In the meantime he could refer me to a psychiatrist so that I could get some medication that would help me sleep. I made the appointment with the psychiatrist and in fifteen minutes he wrote me a prescription for sleeping pills and anti-anxiety medication. That little voice spoke again and said, "You don't need this, don't take the medication; what you need is time to be still."

I had taken more time off from work than I should, and I knew I had to make a decision. Do I go back to my job and take care of other people's business, or do I take the time I need to take care of my business, my life? At the time it was the hardest decision I had to make, but looking back it should have been so easy with everything that was happening. Even as I write this, I think "How could it been such a hard decision to make?"

I bet you are struggling with a decision right now. This is my advice, especially as it relates to work: We are here on this planet first and foremost to love; everything else comes after that.

Yes, I loved my job, but at what expense? I was so unbalanced. I did everything for the company, and rarely did I put the love for myself first. That decision to take time off for me was the most amazing gift I could have given to myself.

It was through that time off from work that I was able to travel the world and finally get properly diagnosed. It was not solved with anti-anxiety medication, and everything to do with the proper food and correct chemistry functioning in my body. I met truly amazing people doing great things in this world, especially relating to health and wellness. I had the opportunity to work on Oprah Winfrey's "Lovetown" show. I had the opportunity to go to the Ellen show. I had time to spend with my dear friend Kate and help with her daughter Avrie, who was battling cancer. I spent time with my dad and family. I fell in love with David, the most amazing man I have ever met. I moved to Australia with him where I met the doctor who would eventually cure me of Hoshimoto's, PCOS, and hypothyroidism. I learned that money is great, but time, love, and laughter are the most precious gifts on the planet. And when making a decision now, I have the winning formula:

Love God
Love me
Love others
\+ Love my work
____
Happiness and health

Chapter 38

Hello gorgeous

by Kim Becker

When my husband and I answered the calling to start a business that would provide complimentary makeovers to women battling cancer, we had a decision to make. We could stay running the successful salon that we had owned for eight years, or we could give up what we knew and follow a dream that was placed on our heart, a dream to do something that had never been done before. Now, I believe in God, and I believe that he directs my steps, and I believe that he placed this dream on my heart. But I also believe that we are all given free will. Even though I felt that this was something I was supposed to do, I had a decision to make. I could stay where I was and remain comfortable, or I could follow what I thought was a crazy dream and venture into the unknown.

We took the chance and decided to venture into the unknown. And believe me, plenty of people considered this a crazy dream. My husband had lost his job at a large retailer in our area, and we had a three-year-old son. I think the hardest thing about making this decision was that no one we were close to had ever taken a chance like this, to leave what I felt was a normal life in order to follow a big dream. We had no one to use as a model. We were trailblazers.

So we sold our successful salon to take on a project that we have found is more fulfilling than anything we could have ever imagined.

My name is Kim Becker. My husband Michael and I started an organization in 2005 as our calling. We owned a full-service hair salon in South Bend, Indiana. When we first thought to open the salon, my husband said to me, "I know what we should call the salon. We should call it Hello Gorgeous!"

I promptly told him that was the stupidest thing I had ever heard in my entire life, and we were not calling it "Hello" anything. I had been an educator for a West Coast nail company many years before and had been very impressed by a salon there in which I had given several classes. It was a beautiful and elegant A-frame building, all of glass, and they had served champagne and cheesecake to all their clients. It was called Cheveux, which meant "hair" in French, and I had known for the last four years that when I opened a salon I would call it that.

"No, no it will be really cool," Mike said, "because every time you pick up the phone, if you greet the person on the other end with 'hello gorgeous' it would make them feel good." I told him it was dumb and we weren't doing it, mostly because the name was already picked out.

We opened Cheveux Professional Hair Design and owned it for ten years. We grew the business quite a bit by the time we sold it. As in every business, we had our ups and downs between employees, taxes, wages, utilities, and repairs. But

I found that I just could not find the complete fulfillment I very much needed in the salon. There was just something missing. There was an emptiness that I could not explain.

I thought that maybe there was something missing in me. So, I went to classes to further my education. I trained in Chicago and Miami and New York and I even attended Vidal Sassoon in London, which was one of my dreams. Still I never seemed to find the fulfillment I was looking for. I became an educator for the color line that we used in our salon at the time, and I did a lot of traveling for them teaching classes. And many of the salons that I instructed on this particular color line were in downtown Chicago. Top salons in the industry were asking for me as their instructor; still, I was not finding the fulfillment I was looking for.

I thought maybe a change would help. So we moved our salon across town, from one location to another, and tripled our size. We expanded our services and, over a few years, grew to fourteen hair stations with stylists and colorists from beginner to master, massage rooms, tanning beds, nail and pedicure rooms, esthetics room, and multiple office staff. We did constant promotions, like referral programs, product sales for holidays, back-to-school specials for product and services, and "The Boss Is on Vacation" sales. We had thousands of clients and did a great business. Yes, it was coffee and mints, rather than champagne and cheesecake, but a wonderful salon regardless.

And still the emptiness was there. That is the only way I can describe it, just emptiness.

In 2005 on a trip back from Indianapolis, Indiana, Mike and I were talking as our son Seth slept in the back seat of the car. I talked with Mike about that same thing that I had felt for a year or more—I just felt like there was something else that we should be doing. I thought there was a higher purpose for us. Suddenly I looked at him and I said, "I know what we're supposed to do!" Mike's eyes got big, and he listened intently as he drove, because he, too, was kind of down on our salon. It had been so much work all the time, for so many years, and it seemed like we just couldn't get it to where we thought it should be. He was looking for a higher purpose as well.

We're supposed to have a mobile day spa, a mobile salon that will cater to cancer patients."

"Wow," Mike said. "That is unique. Wow."

"A place that will be a wonderful and peaceful sanctuary for them, a palace on wheels that will go to their curbside and pamper them with spa services and make them feel like a queen for a day."

"Yes," he said smiling, "that sounds amazing."

I told him we would offer these nurturing services to women with cancer: facial, manicure, pedicure, makeup, and hair styling. I said that we could travel around Indiana doing these makeovers, making hundreds of women happy and change their lives forever.

"Yes!" he said again, louder. Mike was smiling more broadly with each idea, thinking of the positive impact we could make on all these people.

"And . . ."

"Yes?"

"AND . . ."

"YES?"

"And . . . and all the services we would provide these women would be free," I said. "We will charge them *nothing!*"

I watched all the color slowly leave his face.

"Kim, how are we going to *pay* for this? How can we make a living for our family?" he asked.

"I don't know. I don't know how it's going to happen, but I know it's what we're supposed to do." We spent the next several miles in the car with me trying to convince him that this is what we were supposed to do. I could tell Mike was not buying into it, but being the supportive husband that he is, he stopped at a bookstore in Kokomo and went inside the store to buy me three or four different books on women and fund raising, women and nonprofits, and grant writing for dummies—anything he could find that would make this dream come true. He knew that once I set my mind to an idea that there was little chance in changing it.

I spent the next hour talking about this and how we would make it happen. Mike was not saying much and changing the subject every chance he got. About thirty miles from home our son woke up, and we decided to take him into a play area so he could stretch his legs a little bit. As we were sitting there talking I looked at Mike and said, "You know what. *This* is supposed to be called Hello Gorgeous! When these women feel the way that they do during their fight with cancer, that's how they deserve to be greeted. That's what they deserve to hear."

He still wouldn't talk to me about it, and it took me several months to convince him. We held onto the salon for another year and then sold it to concentrate our efforts fully on Hello Gorgeous! Since then Mike has worked six days a week, twelve hours a day at this for the last eight years. I work three days a week as an independent stylist, in the salon we sold to pursue this dream, supporting our family as God unfolds this enormous and amazing journey in front of us. Every woman we are able to help teaches us something. The hugs and tears of joy tell us we are on the right path, that we are making a difference. And Mike has told me that because of what he has seen with this project, and what he has learned from these gorgeous women, that even if he never gets paid real money to do this job, he will not quit.

In 2016 we celebrate the ten-year anniversary of Hello Gorgeous! We have two mobile day spas and thirty-four salon affiliates in nine states. We have published two books and have helped hundreds of women feel gorgeous through their cancer journey.

We once met a couple that taught us "you make a decision, and if it's not the right decision, you make another decision." I can honestly say that this was the best decision we ever made, to follow our dream.

Chapter 39

Living in love, awe, and wonder

by Amy Weider

One of the best gifts I have learned over the years is to be open to learning new lessons from life. Lessons can come in many different forms—that still, small voice within us or perhaps a voice from someone close to us. Listening may be difficult at times, but those of us who truly want to learn and grow will listen. Listening to our own inner voice is sometimes the most difficult. Remembering personal growth is a wonderful way to grow into a person of wise character. Consciously learning from others has helped me personally grow. I have also been able to continue to learn from my own mistakes. Mistakes are not always easy to accept or admit, but they are all part of learning how to become a more decisive woman.

One of my favorite lessons I have learned is to love and accept others. This has manifested itself as finding hearts everywhere I look. Having been opinionated over the years from my "faith" upbringing, I was closed minded to different lifestyles. Being a part of my sister's alternative lifestyle and accepting her partners had been difficult in the past. In my own mind I had to understand what I "thought" I believed and what my heart was telling me. It was not a five-minute decisive decision at the time. Learning from others and understanding their truth opened my mind and heart to a whole new world. People need one gift from us—unconditional love. Through my lesson of unconditional acceptance of my sister and her partner, I was open to finding hearts everywhere I looked. It was her wife who taught me that lesson and gave me that gift, for which I am forever grateful. We were on a beach in Florida fifteen years ago when Elke pointed out hearts she would see all around her. Everywhere she looked there were heart shapes, in the clouds, seashells, and rocks. But, there it was, that one special heart that changed everything. As we walked the beach together there was a huge heart made out of sea shells, and carved in the middle of this heart were the words "I love Jesus." This spoke to me in a very special way. For me it was a life lesson, perhaps my first five-minute decisive decision to love and accept everyone. Today I share my hearts with others on social media, who in return touch my heart by saying to me, "I saw this heart and thought of you." Someone, when I least expect it, thinks of me during his or her day. What a gift to receive from others. Life lesson: *unconditional love.*

After my second divorce, I continued to be open to learning from others. It was at this time that I met a very unique man. He was the first person in my life that opened my heart and eyes to so much more than I ever imagined. He became like a sage to me, a word I had never heard of until I met him. The English meaning for sage is: a mentor in spiritual and philosophical topics who is renowned for profound wisdom (shabdkosh.com). I was so hungry for life, my life! I wanted to learn more than what the past fifty years had shown me. Introduced by a mutual friend, I felt safe having an email connection with him. A written connection that would turn out to inspire a side of me I never knew existed. During our communication we wrote about the meaning of our names. My name Amy means "beloved." From there he shared that "beloved is a combination of admiration, love, awe, and wonder, one who others may look up to." He sensed that I was "an admired creator of love, awe, and wonder." I loved that! Something I had always felt but was never able to put into words.

My imagination and creativity became unstoppable. Words in the written context began to flow; it was as if a light was turned on for the first time in my life. I started writing poetry, which became very cathartic for me. I continue to be inspired by love, awe, and wonder, and I am working on writing a book to share with others. My life lesson from Elke, learning to open my heart to see more than just what my eyes would see, was the beginning of something that would continue in my life. Years later my sage's simple communication via email inspired my first poem. As I looked in the mirror, I realized who I saw was not the same person others saw. From this the writing began. Hundreds of poems flowed. The following poems were written a year apart. My personal growth was happening through my friend as he was teaching me to teach myself my own life lessons.

What Do You See

I looked in the mirror and thought, what do you see?
A Woman, a child staring back at me
A second glance made it clear to see
A Woman, a child starting at three
Remembering that first memory of love I received
A child, now a woman way over thirty
What do you see, when you look at me?
A Woman, a child all grown up,
That's what I am supposed to be . . .
Why is it so different from you to me?
I Wonder . . . The love and the awe that others see
Will I ever see the same that they see in me?
It's time to be free and breathe and dare to dream of
All I am and All I can be!

The Morning Mirror . . .

In the morning mirror all I see
Is the beauty that stands before me.
I stand in awe of what I see,
And wonder why it took so long to be.
I look at me and see someone so pretty
How could that be?
Am I seeing myself for the first time,
Has that image always stared back at me,
Am I noticing something so grander to see,
Could it be?
That I actually am embracing the beauty that represents me
Is the outside matching my heart equally?
The Love for others that I have always expressed
I look and I see God's beauty at its best
A gift, I have received finally, after years of striving to be . . .

A personal spiritual journey and a relationship developed with him for over a year. During that time my lessons were always about my personal growth. I didn't always see it that way at the time. I would come to learn that my sage was one of the most influential people in my life. And although I did not want the relationship to end, I knew I needed to walk away from someone I loved very much in order to continue on my own spiritual journey through life. A life lesson I will forever be grateful for. Life lesson: *self love.*

More recently, I have learned a valuable lesson from a new friend, an unexpected connection of two strangers that met chasing their dream. A deep soul connection of two women possibly separated at birth (in a past life) but a connection felt so strongly in this life. Jennifer has taught me many lessons; my latest is the lesson of the "right fit." I suppose the right fit can be used in many areas in your life—making new friends, clothes fitting properly, job hunting, and so much more. For me it was job hunting. It was a great job, and I though I had the perfect qualifications (twenty years experience); yet I received an email saying there were others more qualified. My first thought was, "What's wrong with me?" and then I was reminded it was not the "right fit." Within a few minutes I was able to process all the right reasons why it truly was not the right fit. It was a lesson I received from a sweet friend who taught me whether or not something is a right fit. I believe this is a wonderful way to look at any situation and make a decisive decision. Always remember to ask yourself is it the right fit? Life lesson: *self-confidence.*

One of my own life lessons came from a lack of good judgment on July 4, Independence Day, a day I will never forget. I made a decision to stay and not leave when my heart and gut said to leave. It was one of my biggest mistakes, but it was also one of my greatest lessons. It was my day of freedom, a day of finally feeling a sense of taking my life back, a day of total independence for me. Details are not important, but the positive outcome of learning a life lesson from my own mistakes, priceless! Life lesson: *personal growth.*

There are so many lessons and stories to share. Sharing more lessons someday through my dream of writing my own book encourages me. There is a huge world around us, and everywhere you look there are lessons to be learned. Listening to others may teach you something about yourself you may never have known. And when we make mistakes in life, instead of criticizing ourselves, we need to step out of our own personal box and look at what we can learn. We need to be open to accepting our own faults and weaknesses and persevere towards growing into the best person we can be. No one has arrived there yet. My hope is that you will embrace knowing "Your past is not your future but has taught you to live in the present!" Keep an open mind and learn from others. You just may be amazed at all the life lessons that surround you.

Chapter 40

Everyday influential women

by Nancy Fox

"After all those years as a woman hearing 'not thin enough, not pretty enough, not smart enough, not this enough, not that enough,' almost overnight I woke up one morning and thought, 'I'm enough.'" Anna Quindlen

The opportunity to impact those around us either positively or negatively is a choice. A great place to start is by simply being ourselves—or an improved version of ourselves—coming from a place of love in our hearts rather than from thoughts in our heads.

While developing this book and reading about the life experiences and impact each woman has had on her loved ones and community, I expanded my view of how people are influenced by women everyday through unique experiences. With my awareness heightened, I began to see, hear, and feel the influence and inspiration of the women around me. Included in this chapter are snippets of the stories women shared with me of how they are a decisive woman influencing others as they live their lives with love and purpose.

Each and every woman is enough. Each one of us has a gift that we carry each day—the gift is that we are. It is the gift of embracing the uniqueness within us and in other women. Embrace the influential women in your life, and embrace yourself as an influential woman. The journey editing this book, *Decisive Women*, has done that for me. What are your everyday influential woman stories? Following are some of mine.

My mom

How did my mom do it? Do *what,* you may ask? Survive? No, live her life with laughter, love, and purpose. After her death and through my grieving, I often asked myself the question: How did mom do it? The gravity of the nine-and-one-half-year survival with lung cancer astounded me. While recalling memorable moments I found many instances where mom chose to bring herself to her feet no matter the challenge or tragedy and live another day with dignity and respect. She found the ability to laugh, bring laughter to others, love in spite of not feeling loved, and trust while being betrayed, all with love and her purpose to influence others. Dorothy Nicholson touched so many lives with her grace and sacrifice of her love for others.

The reflection of my mother's life began a journey of reflection on other women who have influenced me throughout my life. One was Mrs. Dwyer, my first grade teacher. The cafeteria was in the basement of the five-room schoolhouse in the 1950s and 1960s. Mrs. Dwyer encouraged me to eat my spinach. I can see that moment like it happened this afternoon. Her encouraging word of tasting the unknown and her spirit of adventure is anchored in me.

My first grade teacher taught more than how to read, write, and do arithmetic.

Diane and ladybugs

Diane shared a story with me on one of my weird emotional days. You know the ones, when you awaken from a clap of lightening out of a great sleeping moment (some say a dead sleep but rarely someone awakens when dead). The whole house of sleeping beauties was awakened by the subsequent roar of the rapid expansion of explosive heated air known as thunder. This abrupt awakening left me with an emotional cloud that surrounded me until my encounter with Diane.

Diane saw my need, asked to give me a hug, and to my refusal prompted me to open the door and squeezed the negative emotions out of me. Shortly after that I recalled the yellow butterfly floating by me earlier that day, which I lovingly call my mother's way of communicating with me. She (the butterfly) was adorned with yellow wings, catching my eye and lifting my spirits. As I described that moment to Diane, I saw her face light up and she said, "Did I ever tell you the ladybug story?"

Diane shared the story of her mother's passing and the ladybugs that were sent. Yes, ladybugs. She described the oozing of ladybugs in the bathroom of her mother's house days after she passed. The ladybug infestation continued for days. Diane kindly gathered the ladybugs up each day and put them out of the window. Much to Diane's despair an exterminator was needed to end the challenge of the daily ladybug pilgrimage.

A scientist may have a logical scientific reason for this phenomenon. However, as women we find meaning in things that are coincidental, known as signs or unexplained happenings, and they help us connect ourselves and our world around us. There is no right or wrong about it because the event, the butterfly, the ladybug, or the description is the service and beauty we offer our sisters when we are in touch with our spiritual selves.

The encounter with Diane beginning with a hug I was resistant to accept and ending with the ladybug story changed my perspective, my mood, and my spirit. That's what our relationships do for us as women. Our sisters show up sometimes when we need them desperately or sometimes when we don't want them interfering. The result is connection, support, and love transferred in spirit.

Ladybugs continue to show up in Diane's life giving her the remembrance of her mother, love, and spiritual gifts.

Debbie, one who never gives up

Debbie has not had an easy life. Debbie chose a husband who had an unstable income so Debbie worked three jobs to pay her bills on time and make sure the family had what they needed. She assisted her husband to get custody of her husband's son when his mom was unable to provide for him. She has been the strength beneath her daughter's wings no matter the consequences of the growing pains of adolescence and young adulthood. Her life hasn't been easy; yet, her love and caring for her family has been worth the struggles and giving of herself.

Dee, a woman of faith

I met Dee when several things were not working out in her life. She told me, "Everyday you are bombarded with situations or things come in like leapfrogs. Don't let the decisions overwhelm you. I put my decisions in prayer. You will never be given more than you can handle. Praise God each day. Remember, we are his voice, his hands, his eyes and his service."

Monte, an advocate

Monte Skall is a dear woman who is tenacious in fighting for Lyme disease patients. She is the director of the National Capital Lyme Association and is instrumental in the political, research, educational, and patient advocacy arena for the prevention and awareness of tick-borne diseases. She leads the nonprofit group with a mission to help fellow Lyme disease patients and to encourage legislation that will help them to receive the health care they need and deserve. She is a decisive woman who collaborates with other organizations to promote health and wellness in the Lyme community.

Susan, guardian angel

Susan was thirty years old with young children and a husband who made her life full. Then came a day she was totally unprepared to face. She found a red, ring blister on her breast. When she pushed on the round circle it felt like a watery-filled blister that moved around. After she fooled with it she experienced pain that was not there prior to her pushing on it. Two days later the red ring blister disappeared.

It was the beginning of a journey that would consume her attention. She immediately went to the doctor who said it was "nothing" but decided to do a baseline mammogram. When she completed the exam, the radiologist met with her, slapped the films on the lighted display, and said, "Looks like breast cancer. Any questions?" Susan's heart sank and she was devastated with the rude, nasty way the possible breast cancer diagnosis was presented to her. The nurse asked her, "Are you okay?" Susan replied, "No really I'm not." She replied, "He's not saying it is." The nurse sat with Susan and talked with her for about twenty minutes before she left the radiology department.

Susan met with the surgeon the next day to review the results, and he rudely said, "I'm sure you have breast cancer and you need to schedule surgery. Before you get to surgery you need to decide if you want a lumpectomy or a mastectomy to take the whole breast. When you go to sleep you will have two breasts, and when you wake up you could be minus one breast." Susan asked, "Do I need to make a decision to have a mastectomy before surgery? Wait a minute. I need more information. This is my life and my body." Immediately, Susan was faced with many decisions and in a state of shock not only from the diagnosis but the way the radiologist and the doctor presented the information.

Susan's grandmother had promised her that when she passed away she would be her guardian angel. Susan recalled her grandmother's words and rested in faith that her grandmother would see her through this life-changing event.

Susan went home and did research. She found a local woman who put her in touch with a breast cancer patient advocate who spent two hours with her on the phone explaining the options, the treatment possibilities, and a host of information. Susan then called for an appointment with a teaching hospital. She discovered the local hospital had outdated equipment that could misdiagnose and give inaccurate information regarding the state of a possible breast cancer lump. Susan learned that she and her doctors could learn more about her suspicious lump before surgery. By choosing Johns Hopkins Hospital, more than twenty people looked at her suspicious area, and a team gave her the scenarios for her treatment. Susan recovered after a journey through breast cancer and working with her team. However, she wasn't finished with her journey with cancer.

Years later when she was enjoying her adult children and grandchildren, she heard the cancer word again. This time her grandson would be the recipient of the diagnosis. She couldn't believe it was happening, and she was afraid for his life. Her family gathered together and prayed for her young grandson who had a huge tumor intertwined on his spine. It had spread to his pelvis and his lungs. His only symptom came on when he suddenly had trouble walking, and he had previously been an active soccer player. Susan felt tremendous guilt that she somehow had contributed to his condition through heredity. She shared her feelings with her daughter and son-in-law. Her grandson's cancer was caused by a basic incorrect DNA replication. As with her cancer diagnosis, she asked many questions, and she shared her journey with breast cancer with her grandson. She told him she felt her purpose for having cancer was to help him with his cancer. "I can help you because I understand the treatment." Her grandson was surrounded by a loving, faithful, knowledgeable family and community, and he journeyed through his diagnosis and was given the "cancer free" status. Susan said that even in the most difficult times he did exceptionally well.

Bea, lover of magical moments

"Taste the rainbow," Bea told me giggling beyond her sides hurting. "What are you talking about?" I asked. Bea is the person with whom you want to hang around. She is infectious. You know that one person who makes you laugh and makes your day no matter what is happening. Bea loves Skittles®, and she could not resist putting some in her jean pocket before walking onto the floor of her job where breaks and boredom are contrasted between infrequent or too often. "No eating on the floor" was a corporate rule. Bea decided to go to the bathroom prior to her shift because bathroom breaks were unpredictable. As she pulled down her pants (sorry for the graphic details) her jean pocket filled with Skittles flowed out onto the floor in front of her. Disappointed from the waste of perfectly good Skittles and the likelihood of not having any left in her pocket, she began to gather them up. When she looked down a little boy was coming out from under the handicapped stall gathering the Skittles as quickly as he could. Bea quickly responded by pulling up her pants, but then she saw the little boy being tugged by his mama back under the stall partition in a push-pull fashion. The little boy would army-crawl under the stall to be pulled back by his mother's fear. And then Bea noticed the little boy was licking the Skittles off the floor! She was appalled (with hysterical laughter throughout the story) that she had caused such a disgraceful act by the little boy and the embarrassment of his mother. She broke into laughter saying, "He tasted the rainbow and who knows what else!"

Bronte, doing "men's" work well

Bronte looks for projects that would traditionally be thought of as men's work or work a handyman would do. Bronte looks at a design or gets an idea, thinks it through, gathers her materials, and builds the flower garden. When she shares her ideas with her father and brother, they discourage her and believe she is incapable of completing the task. With each new task, Bronte continues to be discouraged by them in spite of the fact that they are aware of the projects she completed without their verbal or physical support. Bronte is a decisive woman paving her way to her enjoyment.

Barbara, chef on the bay

Barbara is an everyday influential woman due to her unique skills as a chef. She describes herself as compassionate, having common sense, and learning to be fearless. She was not the best student but has a work ethic that served her in the jobs she held as a receptionist, bartender, and chef. Barbara seemed to be in the right place at the right time with the right mindset. In the late 80s the greed on Wall Street made a specific impact on her, and she ended up volunteering at the James Beard Foundation. Her experiences and skills were enhanced as she had the opportunity to cook for Bobby Flay and Julia Child. She described herself as moving through the land of misfits but ended up cooking on the Food Network. She attributes her experiences to her ability to believe in her decision-making and to be fearless when experimenting with recipes creating sauces and unique flavors, especially with a lack of correct ingredients. Due to her deep connection with family, she returned home to assist her mom through illness. She has met incredible people who believe in her and support her. She now owns her own restaurant. Prior to meeting her destiny at Barbara's on the Bay, she traveled to Italy, learning from an eighty-year-old woman. While cooking over a pot of tortellini, the woman taught her to cook differently from what she had learned from the other chefs. Her three tips for success.

1. People will tell you what to do, but you must be true to your passion and vision.
2. Giving the staff time off to live their lives is important, so that they are focused when they return to do the exemplary work at the restaurant.
3. Retire in a special place doing what you love. For Barbara that place would be Italy.

Margot, teacher of character

Margot is one of the best teachers with whom I have had the privilege of co-teaching young souls to be productive citizens of society. Margot has two rules: Push in your chair, and Don't say "shut-up." Conceptually "Push in your chair" means to take care of your environment and "Don't say 'shut-up'" means to have respect for yourself and others.

She taught a young boy to reach beyond his limited expectations of himself and show her what he learned in his own way with a few words, a picture, or whatever he could express. Prior to entering her class, that young boy would get angry because he felt he couldn't do the work. Margot taught him that his ideas and thoughts were valuable. She didn't do that with just the one boy, but with each child that entered her classroom.

Margot knows how to teach from the heart, finding the needs of the students and having the confidence to teach them what they need to know to grow and contribute. She taught students knowing they needed structure, discipline, fairness, and a belief in themselves. With those character traits she knew children would become their best.

Margie, a confident instructor

I discovered meek and mild-tempered (my impression of her growing up) Margie at an event in my local neighborhood. She was wearing a karate uniform. I began asking her about her booth and the place of karate in her life. She told me about the classes she teaches to children to build their self-esteem and confidence.

"I always liked watching the TV show "Kung Fu" (1972–1975) and hearing its messages, because I was quiet and timid, and I wanted to gain self confidence. Full aggressive sports were out of the question based on my awareness of being a shy, timid person. In the late 1980s, I started learning karate and found encouragement through the instruction. Mark Churchill led the instruction, and I got my second degree in black belt. Mark was diagnosed with cancer in 2009 and continued to teach until the time came that he had to pass on the teaching. He specifically asked me to continue teaching all of his students." Mark passed away from cancer in 2013.

Margie was unsure about stepping out in front of the class and being a leader of the group. After many years of building her self-confidence she knew this would be the next test. Parents search for discipline and ways to build self-esteem for their children. Honored by Mark's trust and belief in her, Margie continues to serve children by teaching the gift that was given to her many years ago. She is recognized locally and nationally for her ability and dedication to children and martial arts.

Jennifer, business and life coach

Jennifer is one of the most decisive women I know. She is talented, quick-witted, personable, and full of self-confidence. Although only knowing her for a few short years, it seems like a lifetime of a close friendship. She knows what she wants, is great at focusing on the positive, and makes decisions with ease. She encourages those around her and makes others smile while making them laugh. Her infectious energy and smile brightens everyone's day. Her gift to others is coaching them through life in a way filled with love and compassion. There is something so genuine about my friend Jennifer—sometimes hard to find in a friend. She knows what she wants and enjoys living life being a very decisive woman.

Stacey's story, in her words

As a little girl, I was diagnosed with Acute Lymphocytic Leukemia (ALL) just a month after my second birthday. My journey through spinal taps, bone marrows, blood transfusions, treatments, and so forth, was "normal" to me. I thought everyone went through what I was going through. At the time, my perception of life revolved around hospitals, doctor visits, and needles. That was my world, my reality, and my identity.

The wondrous thing about being diagnosed with cancer as a child is that the journey of leukemia, needle sticks, doctors' visits, tests, and retests were normal in my eyes.

Receiving an early cancer diagnosis while still forming ideas and an understanding of your world and your identity, means the concept of loss doesn't enter into your perception of the world. When talking to cancer survivors I have learned we experience cancer differently. The meaning I have developed about my cancer experience is very different from other cancer survivors. I accept that I will have a recurrence of cancer while other cancer survivors fight the thought of a reoccurrence. This is not to say one perspective is right and one wrong but to say the experience, expectations, and perception is different.

Christina, decisive from an early age

Christina Alisa Nye came into this world January 21, 1993. From the beginning, Christina ruled the roost as youngest of my three children. Tina's determination became somewhat frightful to her siblings. One morning while fixing breakfast, with all three of my children gathered about me, Scott and Elizabeth earnestly protested, "Tell her, Mom, she can't come with us. She's too little!" Hot indignation puffed up my three-year-old as Tina replied, "I am not little, and I'm BIG!" That was a defining point in recognizing the essence of her character. Tina felt that she was as important as anyone else in her world—size, age, experience, notwithstanding.

She changed schools and changed names, entering sixth grade as Alisa. (She had decided her first name and all its derivations were too common.) By eighth grade she was investigating where to attend a private school in lieu of public, because she thought she could learn better. She recognized no obstacles in her quest and aimed for the best.

I downplayed my fears regarding money and willingly paid the fraction of the tuition not covered by child support.

At graduation, president of the National Honor Society and recipient of the Literary Award, Alisa was accepted into the second college of her choice. Within a month she became convinced it was the wrong choice for her because of the party scene and politically conservative mindset on campus. She became determined to rectify the situation. The College of the Atlantic offered the same amount of financial aid, so without hesitation, Alisa accessed a small sum of money owed to her in the process of withdrawing and headed for Maine. Her progression in human ecology studies included close relationships with friends and professors and extensive international travel. Surrounded by nature on one of the most beautiful places in the world, she grew further in her appreciation for the fragility and beauty of life with its full spectrum of emotions.

Nothing ever has stopped her, and I trust nothing will. Her determination and decisiveness are intertwined with honoring and caring for herself, so that she may be of service to others and thoroughly enjoy life. Alisa does not and cannot avoid pain or suffering, yet by refusing to be driven by fear she will continue to cultivate living life on her own terms. In doing so, I believe that she honors the God within and continues to blossom into her fullest capacities. She has taught me a great deal about living and connecting to my own God within.

Many people claim that one cannot love another unless one first loves and honors one's self. For me, and for many women I know, we were taught to be the givers and caretakers and put others' needs ahead of one's own. Those precepts of how to behave can deter one from following her true heart with a conscious mind. Alisa's capacity to believe in herself, to follow her gut toward living the life of her dreams, inspires me to continue to do the same.

Jacquelyn, my influential decisive woman

The most decisive woman I ever met was my aunt Jacquelyn. As a single mother, she raised twin boys while working two jobs. Leading by example, she wanted to instill in them a spirit of motivation and a strong work ethic. She never made excuses for her situation or the challenges she incurred as a single mother. As her sons grew older, she decided it was just as crucial to show them the importance of a good education, as it was to tell them. As they attended high school, she decided to go to college. It was quite the challenge. After a ten-year period, she was able to graduate with her bachelor's degree from a local university. This accomplishment enabled her to go from working two jobs to one job. She was able to move up the corporate ladder and become a supervisor in the banking industry. Her decisions allowed her to persevere so she could overcome every challenge that life brought her. She ultimately was blessed to see both of her sons attend and graduate college themselves. I honor Jacqueline as *my* influential decisive woman.

Generally women are touching the lives of others each day. Influential women are often teachers who serve children in building their skills and supporting their development. Influential women include doctors, nurses, medical assistants, and other medical providers who serve the sick and the injured. They include police officers serving on our streets bringing a woman's touch to the service of many. They are firefighters who are cross-trained in medicine as emergency medical technicians and paramedics. Numerous women who are social workers, court clerks, and public servants in many capacities influence the lives of people in ways sometimes only the individual or family recalls with gratitude.

- What shows up in your life that moves you spiritually and connects you with your true identify of self, love, purpose, and meaning?
- Who is your everyday influential woman? Why is she influential in your life? What impact has she had on you in designing your destiny?

Chapter 41

Your decisions, your destiny!

by Nancy Fox

"People will forget what you said. People will forget what you did. But people will never forget how you made them feel."
Maya Angelou

Designing decisions will ultimately shape a plan for your life—in reaching for the best you can be. The impact you have on yourself and others along the way will be mostly positive because you will be in the best form of yourself. Gratitude and graciousness come simply when you have designed your life. Designing your life provides a path but not a guarantee that the path will go as planned.

The design for your life evolves over time with the change of your belief system, which is the core of your direction and purpose. The benefits that you want at twenty years of age versus the benefits you want at forty or fifty are vastly different. The actions that you take during the varying ages and stages of life are based on your experiences and expertise. Some people are born with a thought process and focus on how they can serve. Others are born with a focus on how they can learn what the world has to offer, so they can create something for others. Some of us meander through our lives discovering ourselves and impacting those around us simply because of who we are at the core of our being. The results of our lives, whether the positive or negative moments that encompass it, contribute to the progression of the era we live in. As Elizabeth Gilbert, author of *Eat, Pray, Love,* transformed her life through exploration, she discovered herself while shedding the expectations of herself and those around her. She became quiet and explored and discovered many things, especially her perspective. Living in the present and appreciating the moment with gratitude for the ones who guide us, walk alongside us, and those that may follow us is a gift to acknowledge and embrace. Gilbert wrote, "In the end, though, maybe we must all give up trying to pay back the people in this world who sustain our lives. In the end, maybe it's wiser to surrender before the miraculous scope of human generosity and to just keep saying thank you, forever and sincerely, for as long as we have voices" (p. 334). Are you saying thank you to the many who have led you to this place in life? Are you a woman who is going to be on someone's list that is giving a thank you? This is your life. You design the decisions: the Beliefs, the Benefits, the Actions, the Results, and the Service for yourself and others.

Your life, your decisions, your destiny.

Questions for thought

Reflect on what you have gained from reading this book and either start or continue on your path to designing decisions. Break the BARS of the past and ignite the BARS of your future, designing your life the way you desire. It is through action that you will spread your influence in your community and possibly the world. Your influence is going to happen with or without your conscious vision and design. Begin to make that vision and design by answering the questions below and discovering more about you in the process. Make your life a conscious design towards your chosen path. Jot down your notes in the margin or on some paper.

What women influence or inspire you?

1. Research some of the women mentioned in chapters 3 and 4 or find a woman who enlightens you by her *thinking* or her *doing* that demonstrates her belief system.

- Who is on your list?
- What beliefs does she demonstrate?
- What actions does she take and why?
- What results has she received from her actions?
- Who has she served by her thinking and especially her actions?

2. Think about other women who inspire you.
   - What are the character traits of the women you find interesting, inspirational, and influential in your life?
   - What type of business, organization, or cause do they support or run? Who surrounds them? Who are their sponsors, connections, or associates?
   - What character traits do you have, or would like to have, in common with the women that you admire or connect with today?
   - What do the businesses, organizations, or causes you associate with tell you about yourself? Your beliefs? Your desires?
   - Are you on the journey that aligns with your desires, your beliefs, and your destiny?

3. Who is your everyday influential woman? Why is she influential in your life? What impact has she had on you in designing your destiny?

4. What shows up in your life that moves you spiritually and connects you with your true identify of self, love, purpose, and meaning?

Your path ahead

1. Work on making your life exactly as you want it to be.
   - In what areas of your life do you want to see improvement?
   - What do you want? How will you benefit? Who else will benefit?

2. Take some time to reach into your soul and find the truth about what you want. How do you want to feel? Explore

your childhood dreams. Experience the things that make you happy and you describe as fun.

- How will you benefit?
- Who else will benefit?

3. Think of all the possibilities how your presence can impact someone's life.

4. As you look to the notable women in your life, how did they get where they are at this point of their lives? What action(s) did they take?

5. Now ask or interview the woman you chose, to describe her path to her destiny. Does she answer the question in the way you perceived or does she have a different response?

Design and celebrate

1. Take the next steps to design your decision-making and get the results you want.
   - Are your results aligned with your beliefs, your desired benefits, and your actions?
   - What results have you received from actions taken? Did your beliefs support your desired benefits? Were the results a direct link to your desired benefits? If not, why do you think your results did not meet your desired benefits? Did you take the actions needed to get the desired benefits?

2. Celebrate your contribution.
   - Think of the immediate impact on the people you serve through utilizing BARS.

- What direction or path may have been planted in the person or persons you serve and in yourself because you chose to consciously take action?
- How do you feel about your destiny and the legacy of your life?

About the authors

Dr. Nancy Fox

General editor and writer

Dr. Nancy Fox, an educator with twenty-five years experience, served as general editor for *Decisive Women* and also contributed several chapters. The recognized author of *Hide-and-Seek: No Ticks, Please* (2014), *No Ticks, Please/No Garrapatas, Por Favor* (2015), *Lyme Disease Prevention Education and Awareness K–12 Curriculum* (2015), and *The Parasite Convention* (2016), is a national board certified teacher, life strategist, and speaker. She is a featured radio guest, has appeared on Fox News, and is a speaker for several Lyme disease support groups throughout the United States.

Fox also is the author of *Tick-borne Diseases: An Evaluation of a Lyme Disease Prevention Education Program for Eight, Nine, and Ten Year Olds* (2009). Fox has taken her skills and experience to create a K-12 Lyme Disease and Tick-borne Diseases Prevention Education & Awareness Curriculum collaborating with experienced certified teachers. She has collaborated with several women authors to create a guide for decision-making through real-life experiences and in celebration of the female spirit. Connect with Dr. Nancy at www.drnancyfox.com.

Dave Elliott

Writer of the foreword

When it comes to making sense of the often mystifying topic of relationships, Dave Elliott is an international relationship coach who breaks down complex concepts into easily understandable principles and practices. Whether he's working one-on-one with a client, being interviewed by the media, writing an article that goes viral on the internet, or creating another relationship product, his advice is right on target because he tells it like it is and breaks it down in simple terms.

As a result of his skills and results in relationship transformation, Elliott has shared his expertise on TV and radio and has appeared live on stage. He's the author of *The Catch Your Match Formula*™, a book that helps singles finally find success with online dating by creating the kind of dating profile that gets results (http://catchyourmatchbook.com). In addition, Elliott is also a highly sought-after expert blogger on popular relationship websites. Lastly, he's the creator of The ManMagnetics Formula™—a free website that teaches women the nine secrets that will bring out the very best in men so they can avoid settling for their worst. You can learn all about it at www.manmagnetics.com com or check out Elliott's website at www.legendaryloveforlife.com.

Denver Beaulieu-Hains

Denver Beaulieu-Hains is a public affairs professional with twenty years of experience working as a spokesperson, media consultant, and planner for the military and the federal government.

A survivor of sexual abuse and domestic violence, Beaulieu-Hains weaves media savvy and expert communication skills into stirring, enlightening, and transformational real-world stories and talk designed to uncover solutions for common challenges associated with career, communication, wellness, and finances for all ages. She shares practical easy-to-apply strategies for breakthrough and change. Beaulieu-Hains has a master of science in administration with an emphasis on organizational development and leadership, and a bachelor of arts in speech communications and journalism. Beaulieu-Hains is a native of the Washington, DC metropolitan area and has three adult children. She can be contacted at denverb@hotmail.com

Kim Becker

Kim Becker is an award-winning author and the founder of Hello Gorgeous! of HOPE, Inc., a nonprofit organization that creates a red-carpet experience for all women battling all cancers, providing full spa, ambush-style makeovers in one of their thirty-six-foot mobile day spas or by one of their partnering affiliate salons across the United States.

Becker has been a hairdresser for more than twenty-five years and was a salon owner for ten years. Through the nonprofit, Becker is a business woman, fundraiser, event planner, educator, public speaker, author, public relations person, and the face of Hello Gorgeous! She was awarded the Spirit of Women Award in 2011, a Coaches Versus Cancer Inspirational Award in 2013, and a national Point of Light Award in 2015.

Becker and her husband, Michael, received the Mom`s Choice Award for their first book, *Hello Gorgeous! A*

Journey of Faith, Love, and Hope, published by Corby Books. Their newest book, *I Promise to Put My Lipstick on When I Get There,* is an indispensable how-to beauty book for all women battling all cancers. They have been married for twenty years and thrive in Indiana with their son, Seth, and a pug named Sam. To donate or nominate a woman for Hello Gorgeous! services, go to www.hellogorgeous.org.

Dianne Burch

Dianne Burch is an author, speaker, storyteller, and passionate animal advocate.

For twenty years, she was active as a business owner, creative event planner, and community service board member. In 2010, she made a life-altering decision to combine her professional skills and her passion for rescue animals. With the help of partner and coauthor, Michael Fredrick, World of PawsAbilities was created as a marketing and publishing firm intent on helping to raise the next generation of responsible pet ambassadors through education, entertainment, and community involvement.

MaxNificent! The Polka Dot Pyrenees is the first book in a planned series of children's picture books that pair a traditional style children's story followed by related educational materials about shelter animals, pet responsibilities, and fun pet facts. Book events are planned to create awareness for rescue groups through fundraising, humane education, and adoptions. "These mutts are on a mission!" Visit www.muttmission.com.

Sandra Champlain

The fear of dying led author Sandra Champlain on a fifteen-year journey to find evidence of the afterlife. She conquered her fears when she determined that there is sufficient proof that we don't die. Combined with healing information about grief and tools to live a powerful life, her book *We Don't Die—A Skeptic's Discovery of Life After Death* quickly became a #1 international bestseller. She is the subject of a documentary film titled *We Don't Die* and host of the *We Don't Die* radio show.

Champlain is the owner of Kent Coffee and Chocolate Company in Connecticut, which she began in 1991. A Culinary Institute of America trained chef, Champlain and her mother operate Marion's Hospitality, providing meals to race car drivers and crew members in the United SportsCar Championship.

As a highly respected speaker, author, entrepreneur, and television and radio show guest, Champlain believes every dream is possible. She is committed to making a profound difference in the lives of others. Champlain lives in Byfield, Massachusetts. Visit www.sandrachamplain.com, www.wedontdieradio.com, www.wedontdie.com.

Melinda Cooper

Melinda Cooper is CEO and creator of *Living the Dream* magazine and visibility consultant of *la femme* magazine. Cooper lives her dream working with others to build their businesses and expand their reach. Cooper speaks to various audiences about making the decision to "Live Your Dream" through business and life.

Cooper worked for more than eighteen years with a large government agency in various positions such as employee/labor relation specialist, paralegal for the regional law office, and congressional liaison. Armed with a BA degree and life full of experience, she walks into the arena fully equipped to serve others who are ready to walk forward living their dream. Cooper started her first business in fashion for children and teens at the age of sixteen and sold it to a national clothing chain owned by Merry-Go-Round Enterprises, Inc. Cooper has been in various businesses while working her career with the government agency until 2008, when she walked away to live her dream. She is a firm believer of helping others reach their dreams and works with them to grow their businesses. Cooper is opening wide her next door of opportunities for others who are now ready to work with her on the next adventure. Contact Melinda Cooper at Twitter and Facebook.

Dr. Kyla Dillard

Dr. Kyla Dillard grew up in the Ouachita Mountains of Arkansas and lives in London, Ontario, Canada. She is currently in her twentieth-ninth year of practicing veterinary medicine. Her business card reads: Kyla J. Dillard, DVM; Veterinarian, Comedian, and Political Catalyst. Due to the comments received on this story, "all around badass" may be added to that list. For a more detailed version of story, including photos and videos, go to http://www.kyladillard.com and click on "Repairing My Own Leg after an ER Visit Went Wrong."

Katrina Tse Elliott

Katrina Elliott has been blessed to travel the world extensively while teaching personal development skills that she acquired firsthand while working for some of the masters in the field and their companies—names like Anthony Robbins, Brian Tracy, Loral Langemeier, Alison Armstrong, and John Demartini. After her own four-year-long *Eat Pray Love* journey, she married Dave, who wrote the foreword, and together they share a legendary love for life.

A native of Australia who is a retired police officer and lawyer, Elliott also gives back by traveling around the globe working with groups and individuals supporting Anthony Robbins events. Contact: International Love Coach & Property Investor, Katse999@gmail.com.

Elayna Fernandez

Elayna Fernandez, known worldwide as The Positive MOM, is a best-selling author, award-winning success guide for moms, and international keynote speaker.

Recognized as Best Marketer, Mom Entrepreneur of the Year, Best Latina Lifestyle Blogger, and one of the top 100 Latina influencers in the United States, she is a Certified Guerrilla Marketing Master Trainer and creator of the Guerrilla Positioning System (GPS) for Mompreneurs. Fernandez is a Certified Passion Test Facilitator and Success Trainer. Her mission is to encourage, empower, and equip moms in their journey to create joy, balance, and success on their own terms without guilt, fear, or being overwhelmed. Her philosophy is "BE Positive and You'll BE Powerful!" To learn about Elayna's success mentoring programs, visit The PositiveMOM.com.

Bobbi Govanus

After a thirty-year career in retail, selling everything from socks to stocks, with only a computer and a plan, Bobbi Govanus launched her own small business and soon realized that she had discovered a true niche within the computer training industry. Govanus quickly grew that business from the basement of her Minnesota home by listening closely to her customers and providing customized computer training and solutions. The company eventually brokered over 1000 high-caliber computer trainers across the United States and Canada and even served clients as far away as England, Japan, Germany, and India. She grew the company to sales of over twenty million.

In celebration of these and other accomplishments, Entrepreneur Magazine recognized Govanus as their "Home-based" Business Owner of the Year and Minnesota honored her as their Women in Business Advocate. Bobbi speaks frequently on marketing and empowerment topics.

For 2015 Govanus launched the Reinvention Retreat at Sea, bringing speakers, coaches, and authors together to assist attendees who want to make the rest of their life, the best of their life, doing this transformational work aboard a cruise ship. Govanus published her first book in 2014, *How to Pilot When We Were Raised to BE Stewardesses: Reinventing your Life with Passion and Purpose.* This book explores the importance of choosing your own destiny no matter what obstacles you must overcome to do so.

Bobbi currently lives in Haines City, Florida, with her husband Gary. She can be reached at Bobbi@MrktgMaven.com, www.Re-InventionConvention.com, www.MrktgMaven.com.

Bonnie G. Hanson

Bonnie G. Hanson, CPC, is fiercely committed to guiding women to achieve happy and effective high performance lives so they can consistently live from and in their full potential and create long-term, enduring fulfillment. If you are looking for a proven professional who can guide you to the results you desire, look no further! bonniehanson82@gmail.com

Katie Humphrey

Katie Humphrey is an award-winning entrepreneur, professional speaker, and author of *Elizabeth Hazel and the Day of Desires* (Aperture Press), a purpose-based novel for teens. Her mission is to educate an entire generation of young adults to know that through their individual strengths and flaws they hold an incredible amount of worth, value, and purpose. As a speaker, Humphrey captivates and entertains students with her book's message of believing in yourself and making positive choices. She resides in Jacksonville, Florida, with her husband and Scottish terrier. Discover more at www.KatieHumphrey.com.

Lisa Marie Jenkins

Lisa Marie Jenkins is an executive coach, speaker, and founder of Igniting Brilliance—a consulting company specializing in feminine leadership.

Prior to launching her own consulting business, Lisa spent more than twenty years at Fortune 500 hi-tech companies in senior sales and marketing roles, including Cisco, Xerox, and Tech Data. She recently published her first book, *Wake Up, Beauty! It's Not about the Prince*, and is a regular blog contributor to the Huffington Post.

Jenkins is passionate about working with women to find their passion, purpose, and calling to help heal and transform the way we all work, lead, and live. Learn more or connect at LisaMarieJenkins.com.

Tonya Joy

Tonya Joy is a writer, speaker, trainer, and consultant. She is the founder and chief visionary officer of Congruency Guru. https://www.facebook.com/congruencyguru,

Debra M. Lewis

Colonel Debra M. Lewis (US Army Retired) is best described as a pioneer, leadership-engagement expert, and "Infinite-Win" engineer. Building on a foundation of turning challenges into opportunities, Lewis inspires us to bring out the best in ourselves and in others.

Her positive outlook on life is grounded in a clear understanding of extreme adversity and tough situations at every level, to include what any one of us, or any organization, or any country might face.

After joining the first class at West Point (est. 1802) with women, Lewis served in uniform for thirty-four more years, with a remarkable career full of hard-earned and invaluable experiences. After earning a Harvard MBA, Lewis commanded three US Army Corps of Engineer districts, to include leading a three billion dollar reconstruction program during combat in Iraq and working at the Pentagon on 9/11.

Lewis has honed an impressive skill set that continues to grow, able to transform adversity into something far better and to thrive in spite of difficult situations and relationships that pop up along the way. She reminds us that, "Today's challenges are tough enough. Leadership boils down to bringing out the best in everyone. We dramatically improve our lives whenever we stop buying into the myth that bad behavior isn't that bad for us, and start transforming any unhealthy stress in our lives into something better."

Lewis lives in beautiful Hilo, Hawaii, with her husband, Lieutenant Colonel (Retired) Doug Adams. Together they pursue ways to: Live Life to the Fullest, With Love, In Service. They are blessed with amazing parents, siblings, children, grandchildren, and friends.

Natalie H. G. London

Natalie H. G. London is the author of memoir *Lyme Light*, May 2014. She has an audiobook of *Lyme Light* narrated by Natasha Lyonne (2015). She is the Vox/multi-instrumentalist of band HEY, KING! Contact Natalie H. G. London at www.lymelightmemoir.com or heykingband@gmail.com.

Jo-Ellen Marks

Jo-Ellen Marks is a master trainer, inspirational speaker, author, and coach. She has a strong fitness and wellness philosophy that anyone can attain a truly healthy lifestyle simply by taking small, consistent steps toward the goal of health and well-being. She had to put this knowledge to good use after a series of three car accidents left her with an mTBI that was misdiagnosed for more than three years.

Marks has more than twenty years of experience in the fitness, wellness, and coaching fields. Her experience includes a balanced use of multiple disciplines including: motivation, goal setting, mindfulness, and exercise. She brings these skills together into a unique training philosophy of three steps, "Stop, Choose, Start," that will help you meet your personal goals. Marks currently works for a large medical company in New Jersey as the director of fitness programming for seniors. Contact Jo-Ellen Marks at fitnessjo@gmail.com.

Dorothy Nicholson

Dorothy was an administrative assistant for Luke Nicholson's Plumbing, Heating, and Electric Company for twenty-five years. She was the co-owner of Taylor's Island Campground from 1980–1987. Nicholson was proud of her role as wife to Luke Nicholson of sixty years and mother of five children.

Marissa O'Neil

Marissa O'Neil is an award-winning author, speaker, and founder of Wellness and Beyond: From Pain to Purpose, an integrative wellness company in Santa Monica, California. With more than sixteen years of experience in the health and wellness industry, O'Neil specializes in relieving pain physically, mentally, emotionally, and spiritually to improve her clients' quality of life. She works with individuals to discover the physiological source of their discomfort as well as addresses the accompanying cognitive, emotional, and spiritual thoughts and beliefs that contribute to the physiological pain. She then engages her clients in a series of activities that teach them how to restore their body's natural balance and empowers them to live a more productive and fulfilling life.

O'Neil has a degree in kinesiology from Colorado College. She began her career in New York City as the medical director at La Palestra—a center for preventative medicine, where she closely coordinated clients' healthcare with orthopedic surgeons, physical therapists, chiropractors, nutritionists, internists, masseuses, performance specialists, and behavioral psychologists. She moved to Santa Monica, California, in 2007 to develop a new performance training center called Core Performance, with the philosophy of integrating mindset, nutrition, movement, and recovery. Later she pioneered Corporate Health & Productivity Programs within Fortune 500 companies including: Google, Intel, and LinkedIn. Over the years O'Neil has worked with a clientele that includes Olympic gold medalists, professional athletes, actors, entrepreneurs, adolescents, as well as special populations including orthopedic ailments, cardiac care, weight management, and pregnancy protocols.

To learn more about O'Neil's award-winning book *Coastal Inspirations: Drawing Beauty and Meaning from the Sea* visit www.coastalinspirationsbook.com. To learn how you can work with her to relieve your pain visit www.marissaoneil.com.

Leslie Petruk

Leslie Petruk is a child & family therapist and parenting expert. She has worked with children, couples, and families to help them lead more connected and compassionate lives since 1996. Petruk and her husband of twenty-five years live in Charlotte, North Carolina, with their three children, where she owns and runs her counseling center, the Stone Center for Counseling & Leadership. Her greatest joy is her husband and three children. Her fourteen-year-old son has special needs; she along with her two daughters have been blessed with ADHD, and her husband is dyslexic! So, suffice it to say—she knows the challenges she speaks of. Petruk loves sharing "this was not one of my finer parenting moment" stories when she teaches and coaches parents, and with three children she'll never run out of stories to share.

Petruk was a contributing writer for *Little Ones Magazine* for eight years and is often interviewed for news stories related to various parenting topics and has been interviewed for articles in publications such as *Ode Magazine, the Huffington Post, SheKnows.com, Charlotte Parent,* and many others. She is the author of the upcoming book, *OMG! I Sound Just Like My Mother: How to Parent* Your *Way with Courage, Clarity, and Compassion.* You can find more information on her book website at www.omgisoundjustlikemymother.com or her counseling center page at www.thestonecenternc.com.

Raining Deer

Jeanette Stephens-El is an accomplished author, breast cancer thriver, and Community Ambassador to Susan G. Komen for the Cure—Philadelphia. She served a five-year term as fundraising chair and Race for the Cure cochair with upwards of twelve million dollars raised under her leadership. Stephens-El wrote two books on breast cancer: BC*V—Rites of Passage for Breast Cancer Victors, and 10 Tips to Avoid Breast Cancer (Unless it's in the Genes),* as well as *T-Time: A Rites of Passage Manual for the Adolescent Female* all written under her spiritual/pen name Raining Deer.

A New Jersey native, Stephens-El resided in Miami, Florida, for twenty-four years where she was a contributing writer for several newspapers, served as creator/

editor-in-chief of *Southern Dawn Magazine*, and was publicist for Philip Michael Thomas during and post "Miami Vice." She also was founding director of a writers' workshop, coordinator of the annual Pan African Bookfest & Cultural Conference, and a theatrical producer.

Stephens-El is in demand as a speaker, having addressed events from Miami to New York. Numerous media appearances include CBS-3 News, NBC-10 News, ABC News.com, the *Philadelphia Tribune,* Princetontv.org, the *Atlanta Constitution*, Boomer Living.com, *WOW Magazine*, and a 2015 iHeartMedia breast cancer forum on WDAS-FM Radio. Featured in the 2010 book, *Forever Young at 50+*, Stephens-El is a member of the International Women's Leadership Association, was named a 2012 Woman of the Year by the National Association of Professional Women, and coauthored the 2012 Gratitude Book Project. Stephens El attended Miami-Dade College in Miami, Florida, under a Knight Scholarship. See more at www.linkedin.com/pub/jeanette-stephens-el/17/b1/41a and www.authorhouse.com/rainingdeer.

Virginia Rector

Virginia Rector has masters degrees in special education and city and regional planning; she is currently participating in a masters program of theological studies in ministry and culture. She has worked in public school special education programs and served in ministry support in several states. She has served as the literacy coordinator for Save the Children in Spartanburg, South Carolina, executive director for communities in schools, and director of career services at the University of South Carolina Spartanburg.

Rector is a consulting advisor of the Daughters in Christ Ministry & Marriage Enrichment Ministry at Pilgrim Baptist Church, also a charter member and former graduate advisor of the Rho Tau Chapter, and vice president—Epsilon Beta Omega Chapter, and currently general member of Alpha Kappa Alpha Sorority, Inc. She is the former first vice president of the Interdenominational Association of Ministers' Wives and Ministers' Widows of Wilmington and vicinity, as well as a member of the Delaware Association of Ministers' Wives and Ministers' Widows. She has a passion for mentoring teen girls and young women. Rector can be reached at vrector2003@yahoo.com.

Dell Scott

Dell Scott, also known as "Diva Dell," is the CEO of Dell Scott Enterprises and Divacoutoure. As an international speaker, she ministers with the strong desire to see women become empowered by unleashing their inner brilliance. Scott's purpose and passion is to show women how to believe in themselves and realize that they are created in excellence. She reveals to women the importance of image in order to succeed in their personal lives as well as their careers. With a calling to also impact women at a younger age, Scott utilizes her skill set to mentor female youth in local forums.

Being a fashion designer and stylist, Scott shows women how to transcend their inner beauty to the outside for all to see. She finds joy in seeing women further enhance the beauty they already possess. Her fashion collection, The DS Collection, is femme fashion for the woman who knows the brilliance she possesses.

Scott is also the visionary and creative force of Divacoutoure, an online "Tour de Fashion" boutique with various fashion retail products and services. It is her company's mission to see women become empowered to unleash their "Inner Diva" through the art of exquisite fashion. Divacoutoure is a "Tour de Fashion" boutique with various fashion retail products and services.

As an author, Dell expressed the challenges of being a kingdom wife, mother, and entrepreneur. This message was brought to the world in her coauthored *MRS. BOSS, Vol 1: Memoirs of Divas that Hold It Down Fearlessly.* Her new release, *The Undiscovered Jewel: Realizing the Brilliance that Lies Within*, taps into the revelation that women need to know that they are precious and brilliant in order to reveal their true selves to the world. She is the fashion columnist for *K.I.S.H. magazine* and authors the fashion blog, Fab Factor. Scott resides in Clayton, Deleware, with her husband Jermaine and two children, Jasmin and Jermaine II. Connect with Scott at www.dellscott.com or www.divacoutoure.com com. She also can be reached at 1-800-804-0194.

Lhea Scotto-Laub

Lhea Scotto-Laub is the president and owner of Quantum Business Group, Inc., Massapequa, New York, a professional writing service specializing in resume writing, interview coaching, and business support. Scotto-Laub has composed more than fourteen thousand resumes, bios, cover letters, and personal statements since 1988. Additionally, she has placed more than one thousand candidates in her career.

In the volunteer arena, Scotto-Laub is the past president of the Long Island Center for Business & Professional

Women, a thirty-five year premier women's networking organization. She has chaired several committees and co-established their speed-networking event. Additionally, Scotto-Laub served as a board member of the Long Island Women's Business Council for several years and was a former board member of the US Women's Chamber of Commerce, where she contributed to the launch of the first diversity awards on Long Island in 2004.

Scotto-Laub has cochaired and sat on the Women of Distinction committee for the March of Dimes for more than seven years, which strives to improve the mortality rate of babies and expectant mothers through fundraising and awareness. From 2004–2006 she wrote a monthly a column for LIwomen.com, spotlighting a Long Island businesswoman who made a significant difference. In 2010 she was honored with the Presidential Achievers' Award by the Long Island Center for Business and Professional Women. She received citations from New York Governor Andrew Cuomo and New York State Councilwoman Dorothy Goosby for leadership, humanitarian efforts, and volunteerism. From 2009–2014 Scotto-Laub was an active member of Rotary, an international organization that serves humanity on a local and international level. She was secretary of the West Hempstead Rotary Club and has been involved in the Rotary Youth Leadership Awards committee on Long Island.

Scott -Laub was a single-parent for more than twenty years of 3 sons and has two grown step-children. While raising her sons, she was determined to raise educated, kind young men who possess a strong work ethic, integrity, and a humanitarian heart. www.success-resumes.com or www.822jobs.com

Sally Stap

Sally Stap is a writer living in Kalamazoo, Michigan. She began writing after brain surgery and a long, ongoing recovery brought her information technology career to a halt. Struggling with head pain, facial paralysis, and single-sided deafness, she turned to writing to capture her life-changing experience. In addition to authoring her memoir *Smiling Again: Coming Back to Life and Faith After Brain Surgery* (2014), she was a contributing author to *Imagine This! An ArtPrize Anthology (2013), The Transformation Project* (2013), and *Faithwriter's Trials and Triumphs* (2014). She blogs regularly at www.smilingagainbook.com and www.sallystap.com.

Laura Steward

Laura Steward is a sought after speaker, business advisor, radio host, and author. After building and selling her highly successful technology services company she started Wisdom Learned, LLC, a company dedicated to educating leaders based on experience and wisdom learned in the trenches.

Steward is the author of the award-winning #1 international best-selling book *What Would a Wise Woman Do? Questions to Ask Along the Way*, which was on the Amazon Woman in Business best-seller list for more than ninety weeks and continues to hit best-seller lists around the world.

Through her weekly broadcast radio show *It's All about the Questions,* keynote speeches, books, seminars, training, and one-one sessions, Laura's mission is clear—help people get off autopilot and create amazing, successful lives. Contact Laura Steward at www.LauraSteward.com, Laura@LauraSteward.com, or 772-202-2183.

Tammy Studebaker

Tammy Studebaker is a marketing representative for a health and wellness company. She is on the board of directors for the Lyme Disease Association of the Eastern Shore of Maryland and runs a support group in Centreville, Maryland. Her daughter has multiple food allergies, and her son has celiac disease. Studebaker has presented and offered cooking classes at Whole Foods over the past several years along with blogging for several different publications. She also presents motivational programs to teens and presents programs to adults on the process of accepting their "new normal" and surviving illnesses. Her entire family, including herself has battled tick borne disease. Contact Tammy Studebaker at healthycentreville@gmail.com.

Irene Tymczysyzn

Irene Tymczysyzn is a promoter, connector, and motivational speaker to all who come in contact with her as well as on stage for audiences around the globe. Irene spent a majority of her career traveling the world in search for the best consumer products and best innovators on earth. She also worked for the Walt Disney World Co. where her passion for personal development and human behavior was born. Throughout her career traveling the world for the best products and people on earth she used the principles of personal development and human psychology to keep her and her teams operating at a peak performance. In 2011, ten major life events within a period of a couple months, changed the trajectory of her life forever.

Now, not only does she speak from the heart and is a walking example of how making a decision for your best self can change lives, Tymczysyzn embodies her mantra from the soul of "Plenty of Time, Plenty of Money, Plenty of Health and Plenty of Laughter" for each and everyone of us on this earth. No joke.

Dianne Watson

Dianne Watson is a photographer and author. She is the CEO of Diane Watson Photography. She is currently working on a book about disaster preparation with a focus on saving the $30,000 after the storm. Her fine art photography has been displayed in the Vargas and Harbin Gallery and the Hudgens Gallery. She has held management positions with eastern airlines, continental airlines, and Intercontinental Hotels Group. Contact Dianne Watson at dkwphotos@gmail.com.

Amy Weider

In search for inner peace, purpose, and self-esteem Amy Weider relied on others to fill her heart with love. After embracing a renewed faith and filling the desperate void of being alone, she suffered many of the same challenges women of all ages face today.

Weider is dedicated to inspire others to recognize the love that is within them, the awe of the beautiful life that surrounds them, and the wonder of life's gifts that can amaze them. She is currently writing a book titled *Living Life Filled with Love, Awe and Wonder*, a love story of finding true love for oneself by letting go of expectations of what we have seen, heard, and been taught our entire life and following our inner passions.

Weider is an entrepreneur and fulfilled her life's dream by

receiving her bachelor of science degree in health science at the age of forty, graduating summa cum laude. She enjoys pursuing her "love" of traveling, sees the "awe" of the beauty that surrounds her through her photography, and the "wonder" of connecting with people and building relationships with total strangers. A mother of two successful adult children, a grandmother of four, and a caregiver for her elderly parents, Weider resides in Rochester, New York. Amy also enjoys writing on her blog Love Awe Wonder http://loveawewonder.com.

Chapter notes

Chapter 5

1. Elizabeth Girvan, "The Strength of Femininity," http://www.huffingtonpost.com/quarterlette/the-strength-in-femininity_b_7186332.html

2. Susan Brownmiller, *Femininity* (Ballantine Books, 1985), Prologue.

3. Anna Pasternak, "Fast Track to Femininity," http://www.dailymail.co.uk/femail/article-1039030/Fast-track-femininity-Why-competing-men-left-women-touch-feminine-side.html

4. Julie Serrano, "Empowering Femininity," Ms. Blog, July 28, 2014, http://msmagazine.com/blog/2014/07/28/empowering-femininity

Chapter 7

1. Sharon Begley, "The Science of Making Decisions," Newsweek Tech & Science, February 27, 2011, http://www.newsweek.com/science-making-decisions-68627

2. Anthony Damasio, *Descartes' Error: Emotion, Reason, and the Human Brain* (Penguin Books, 2005).

3. Jacqueline Howard, "Can Science Show Us Secrets of Making Better Decisions?" http://www.huffingtonpost.com/2013/09/01/science-secrets-making-decisions_n_3844400.html

Chapter 9

1. Wendy Lipton-Dibner, *Focus on Impact* (Morgan James Publishing 2016), ix.

Chapter 31

1. Sheri Dew, *Saying It Like It Is* (Deseret Books, 2009), 27.